Unbowed

An Algerian Woman Confronts Islamic Fundamentalism

Khalida Messaoudi

Interviews with Elisabeth Schemla

Translated by Anne C. Vila

PENN

University of Pennsylvania Press

Philadelphia

Originally published 1995 as *Une Algérienne debout*
Copyright © 1995 Flammarion
English language edition copyright © 1998 University of Pennsylvania Press
All rights reserved
Printed in the United States of America on acid-free paper

10 9 8 7 6 5 4 3 2 1

Published by
University of Pennsylvania Press
Philadelphia, Pennsylvania 19104-4011

Library of Congress Cataloging-in-Publication Data

Messaoudi, Khalida, 1958–
  [Algérienne debout. English]
  Unbowed : an Algerian woman confronts Islamic fundamentalism :
Khalida Messaoudi / interviews with Elisabeth Schemla ; translated by
Anne C. Vila.
    p.   cm. — (Critical authors & issues)
  Includes bibliographical references (p.   ).
  ISBN 0-8122-3449-9 (cloth : alk. paper). — ISBN 0-8122-1657-1
(pbk. : alk. paper)
    1. Islam and politics—Algeria. 2. Jabhah al- Islāmīyah lil-Inqādh
(Algeria) 3. Muslim women—Algeria. I. Schemla, Elisabeth.
DT295.5.M4713   1998   98-12254
965.0'0922—dc21   CIP

Unbowed

Critical Authors & Issues
Josué Harari, Series Editor

A complete list of books in the series is available from
the publisher.

To Eugène Mannoni, lord of journalism, and noteworthy passerby

To all the women who have been raped or assassinated by the armed groups of the F.I.S.

To the intellectuals, children, artists, journalists, and other victims of fundamentalist barbarism

To all the men and women of the resistance, who are saving our honor in Algeria

Contents

Translator's Note

The acronyms used in this translation remain in the internationally recognized French form. All acronyms, along with a number of Algerian and French terms and selected sociohistorical references, are explained in the glossary that follows the text. The first time an acronym, term, or reference appears in a chapter, an asterisk is used to guide the reader to the pertinent entry in the glossary.

This English translation transliterates Arabic words and personal names found in the original text according to the French forms used by both French speakers in Algeria and many Western scholars. Place names also adhere to this system unless they are well known in English (for example, "Algiers" rather than "Alger").

I am grateful to Alek Baylee Toumi and to Susan Slyomovics for their assistance in providing information pertinent to the acronyms, names, and other sociohistorical references that appear in this book.

Prologue

The first time I found myself face to face with Khalida Messaoudi, in July 1994, I was impressed. She had just been wounded in the leg by a bomb that had exploded during a democratic demonstration in Algiers, and I sensed that she was going through one of the periods of dejection that all resistance fighters feel at one time or another. She believed that the world was indifferent to the suffering and solitude of Algerian women. The soldierly nobleness of her face gave all the more weight to the words she said to me then: "The veil is our yellow star." Those words were destined to become the title of the interview she gave me a few weeks later for *Le Nouvel Observateur*—an interview that would prove to be decisive for her fight.

It is exceedingly rare in the Muslim world to meet a feminist who is determined to do whatever it takes to prevent fundamentalists from seizing power in her country. Every act of political resistance implies that the person making it has a strong character and strong convictions. I hope that, after having read these conversations, readers will have a greater appreciation of the fervor, the power of conviction, and, finally, the sense of sacrifice that a woman in the land of Islam must have to stand up to Allah's zealots, to refuse the advent of an Islamic state—and to dare to do it, as Messaoudi has, from the inside, despite death threats, in the name of the freedom of women, who are, without question, the true victims of fundamentalism.

Everything Messaoudi represents defies the polarities that are ripping Algeria apart today. She is "indigenous," in that she is a Berber from Kabylia, yet she is also a highly educated intellectual; she is a lay Muslim in a society that is slowly reimposing religious constraints on every aspect of life, from the law to the smallest de-

tails of women's dress and behavior; she is Francophone, Arabo-
phone (classical and dialectal), and Berberphone in a post-colo-
nial Algeria that seeks to stifle dissent by imposing a monolingual
Arabic system of education; she is militant but nonviolent; she is a
democratic republican in a nation where two competing totalitarian camps are struggling for power; and, most important, she is a
feminist—that is, someone who fights to obtain the most basic civil
rights for women—in a misogynous culture that is more and more
hostile to women and obsessed with repressing female rights and
sexuality.

What are the major battles reflected in the testimony Khalida
Messaoudi gives in this book?

Democracy for Algeria. In political terms, Messaoudi occupies an impossible third site. Between the Scylla of the ruling single-party
regime of a military junta tied to the corrupt F.L.N.*, and the
Charybdis of the terrorist fundamentalists who, since 1992, have
been savagely murdering intellectuals, artists, journalists, liberal
professionals of all kinds, girls who refuse the veil, and entire
Berber villages—as the French philosopher André Glucksmann
has put it, the Algerian situation is not a "civil war" but a "war
against civilians"—she belongs to the generation which was born
after Algeria's war for independence (1954–62) and which is at-
tempting to construct a modern democratic state in Algeria.

The Family Code*. On the feminist front, Messaoudi fights against
the Family Code that was passed into law by the F.L.N. in 1984,
eight years before the Islamic fundamentalists began their violent
terrorist campaign to enforce strict observance of *charia** regarding women. Among the Code's edicts are the following: women
are never considered adults under the law; men are always the
heads of their households, and must be treated as such; a wife
must respect the wishes of her husband *and* of his family; women
cannot travel without the approval of a male family member;
women cannot arrange their own marriage contracts unless a
male guardian speaks for them; and women are unable to apply
for divorce.

Islamic fundamentalism. As Fatima Mernissi, the Moroccan feminist sociologist, has underscored, innovation, the freedom to doubt, self-affirmation, any sort of empowerment for women, and the very notion of the individual are all deeply disturbing and threatening to the communal consensus on which Islam's hierarchical, pyramidal male order is based.[1] From the "in-your face" photo on the back cover of this book to her descriptions of the rituals she follows in dressing and putting on her makeup, Messaoudi makes a defiant point of her publicness as an unveiled woman. Her public assertion of femininity thus takes on a militant, resistant connotation in light of the repressive order for women to cover up.

Linguistic repression. Why this book, at this time, in this form, and in French? Given that Algerian (Algerian Arabic, or *faraber*[2]) is a hybrid language that is spoken but not written, writers whose mother tongue is Algerian or Berber are obliged to return to a non-native language, either French or classical Arabic. Moreover, by choosing to relate her story in French, Messaoudi transforms this language of Algeria's last colonizers into an instrument of liberation—a central weapon in her fight against the monolingual Islamist ideology promoted by both the fundamentalists and the F.L.N., which controlled the Algerian government and education system from 1962 until it fell from power in 1991. Messaoudi embraces French, as opposed to classical Arabic, as a way to combat the imposition of a pan-Arabic identity on a culture whose diversity predates its respective Roman, Arab, and French invasions.

When Khalida Messaoudi asked me to write this book with her, I accepted without hesitating because I treasure her friendship: she is as old as her country, and it is her turn to speak about it, for the agony of Algeria is once again seizing hold of the world. Several years ago, Arab writers and intellectuals came together to express their outrage against another *fatwa** in a volume entitled *For Rushdie.* Perhaps, as witnesses to her testimony, free people the world over should publicize their support for this woman warrior,

---

1. Cf. Fatima Mernissi, *The Veil and the Male Elite: A Feminist Interpretation of Women's Rights in Islam* (Reading, Mass.: Addison-Wesley, 1991) and *Women's Rebellion and Islamic Memory* (London: Zed Books, 1996).
2. See "Language in Algeria" in the Glossary.

to counter with free speech the death sentence that has been issued against her, and write back—not just to Khalida, but *For Khalida.*

Elisabeth Schemla
(with Ronnie Scharfman and Josué Harari)

Chapter 1
The "Quite Beneficial" Years

Elisabeth Schemla: It has been two years since you were condemned to death by the Islamic Salvation Front [F.I.S.*]. How were you informed of this death threat?

Khalida Messaoudi: It happened over a period of time. First, in 1992 and early 1993 I got some phone calls in the middle of the night, when I was at home, in the town of Baranès, a middle-class town in the hills of Algiers where I was living. In general, this would occur after a meeting, a demonstration, or a radio program. A voice would say to me: "You're all going to die!" Then, there were some verbal attacks made against me during prayers, in the mosques of the F.I.S. Over the mosque loudspeakers, whose monotonous echoes penetrate into the very center of the surrounding houses, imams would hurl curses at me, describe me as a "woman of delinquent morals" and a "danger to the morality of women," and warn those women who might be tempted to follow my example. One day, one of my old students who lives in Larbaa, sixty kilometers away from Algiers, called me, terrified. She had heard the local imam from her bedroom window, and she told me exactly what he said: "The renegade, the sister of Satan must die! Khalida, return to the faith!" To be honest, I didn't take all this very seriously—until, in the space of a few days, the fundamentalists attacked the leading intellectuals they had targeted, killing them in front of their apartment buildings. That was in March of 1993. I was in Paris at the time undergoing medical treatment. I learned through my sister that they had come to look for me as well, at my home, where they didn't find me, and for a very good reason. In fact, I was lucky to escape from that first wave of executions, and that made me realize that I was on their lists. Unfortunately, none of my friends who were assassinated—and they were all my friends—had this chance. I decided to go back nevertheless, but, obviously, I didn't return to my residence. I began to hide, I stopped working, and I continued to be politically active by working covertly at the center of my movement. Finally, a letter in a handwritten envelope arrived in my mailbox,[1] and my parents forwarded it to me. It was a very official communiqué, photocopied, announcing that I had been condemned to death.

E.S.: Since then, you have always succeeded in escaping from the fundamentalists ...

K.M.: You don't know how right you are! Imagine this: I discovered in an April 1994 issue of *Etabsira*, the news bulletin published by the F.I.S. in London, that I should have died a few days earlier, on March 22, in the evening. The article said that an armed group was resolutely waiting for me in El-Biar, in front of the home of a friend with whom I was planning to stay that night, and that I had not shown up. The information was quite exact: I had indeed changed my plans at the last minute, because I still had work to do. I can't help believing that *baraka** exists, even for secular feminists! God keeps his eye on his own!

E.S.: And that wasn't the end of it ... For example, the last big demonstration of the democrats that you were leading, held in June 1994 in Algiers, was interrupted by a bomb attack. Two people were killed and seventy were injured in the explosion, which was aimed at you and Saïd Sadi*, the president of your movement. You escaped with a small piece of shrapnel in your leg. Anyone else would have given up; but you, you continue in spite of everything to live in Algeria.

K.M.: I have no children, and that changes everything. I only have to worry about saving my own skin. I don't live in the maddening anguish of wondering whether my children will still be alive the next minute, or whether they are going to school, being properly fed and looked after, while I am in hiding. You know, if you don't have a clan around you in Algeria—especially a family clan—it is impossible to survive right now when you have children. Those who are forced to go into exile do so because they don't have that protection, not even the protection of a party or union, and I understand why they leave Algeria. I am fortunate to have both kinds of protection.

1. See "Death Sentence for Khalida Messaoudi," pp. 167–68.

E.S.: Has your family been taking care of you since you've been on the run?

K.M.: Of course, and it's completely natural for them. When you're condemned to death, you no longer have anything: you have to give up your work and move around all the time—every week, practically. You have to find apartments you can hide in, cars to get you from one place to another because you can no longer drive yourself, money for food—in a word, a network. My father, who has a small pension from his job as a mayoral advisor, couldn't have done anything on his own. But those of my seven brothers and sisters who have sufficient means set aside enough money every month to give me the equivalent of what I used to earn as a teacher, more, even. When I need to go abroad for a conference or a political event, they pay my airfare. One day I told them that all this was too expensive for them. They replied: "This is our way of supporting you." They are extraordinary. That, too, is a form of resistance: the shadowy kind, which is discreet, efficient, and determined. My mother stays at home and doesn't get involved in politics, but she is the greatest militant I know! Many of my women friends, who are waging the same fight as I am, aren't so lucky. Some of them have been disowned by their parents or rejected by their husbands. And yet they continue to fight! In my more extended clan, there is even someone who has held a high-level position in the National Liberation Front [F.L.N.*] for quite some time, and who completely disagrees with the choices I have made, just as I disagree with his, but that didn't stop him from sheltering me for awhile. Without the support I've gotten from my family and fellow militants, I would have died ten times over the past two years.

E.S.: You live in Algiers but you are a Kabyle*, and the Kabyle clan can be daunting if anyone threatens one of its members. We saw a case of that during the kidnapping of the singer Matoub Lounès, whose life was saved thanks to it ...

K.M.: If the fundamentalists try to touch one hair on my head, my four brothers, first of all, will take it on themselves to make them pay for it. My uncles wouldn't even have to lift a finger! But if that happened, my entire village would mobilize. The clan spirit of defense is not just an expression with us. It may be for that reason that the Islamists, who once ransacked the apartment of one of my brothers while he was away, haven't tried anything else.

E.S.: Just how afraid are you?

K.M.: I'm a very fearful person, really. I don't want to die and I'm afraid of dying. I believe that one has to be honest with oneself and recognize this kind of feeling. Don't worry—I quite often look at myself in the mirror in the morning and say: "Khalida, you're afraid!" After that point, if the fear gets the better of you, you're screwed. Whether they kill you with a bullet or drive you insane, their goal is achieved. Now, I am not ready to die, neither physically nor symbolically. So I tell myself: "Well, then, you'll have to find the means of overcoming this fear." And I've spent the last two years of my life trying to find those means.

E.S.: What are they?

K.M.: I've learned that there are two traps I must avoid at all costs: the trap of shame and the trap of hate.

E.S.: What do you mean by that?

K.M.: In life-or-death situations like those with which we're faced in Algeria, where the ideological confrontations are very hard, anything goes if you're trying to discredit a political enemy. I'm a political enemy for almost all the opposing forces because I contest the Islamists, the F.L.N., and the military leaders who are now in command, and I call for a real republican democracy in my country. Over the course of several months, the rumors and hateful newspaper articles about me have multiplied. I've heard and read all sorts of claims made against me, coming from all directions: people say that I am a cop, an agent of military security and the government, that I have run off to Canada with the funds of the feminist association I lead, and similarly kind words. Obviously, one can do nothing to fight such slander and libel, and I had bouts of terrible depression for a long while: I would get indignant, it would eat me up inside, and I'd feel degraded. In a word, I was ashamed. And then I realized that if I stayed that way I was done for. So I tried hard to learn how to keep my cool in the face of these attacks. I knew that I had won when, after spending a sleepless night thinking about a certain article that was particularly hurtful, I decided not to respond to it. Since then I have never deviated from this line. I swore to myself that I would never indulge in that kind of verbal assassination. Cheating death begins by not killing yourself, in any way. My father realized how I'd changed. On those rare occasions when we get together, he looks at me and says: "Clearly, all this has knocked some sense into your head."

E.S.: What are you still afraid of?

K.M.: Of madness—the madness that can come from leading a rat-like existence in which you lose all your bearings. I sometimes wonder how we'll end up after it's all over, given that our nerves are so exhausted. Of course, there is also the strain of working covertly, and having to continue in spite of the obstacles and the loneliness. But do you know what it's like to see all your friends kidnapped, taken hostage, and shot down one after the other?

E.S.: Let's go back to those lost bearings, if you don't mind. Which was the most important?

K.M.: My job, and by far. For me, being a math teacher was my entire life. Every aspect of my existence was structured around teaching. I had always been a hard-working person, but I very quickly sublimated the constraint and made work ... a source of pleasure, that's it. When I was deprived of my work, it was as if I no longer had a spinal column. And no longer having a home, a place to have your friends come over or to do those trivial things that you don't think about when you're free—that, too, is difficult. For example, when you get home, you toss your shoulder bag into a corner. The bag has its corner: end of story! It's the same thing for the objects in your bathroom, for everything. And then, if you want to escape from the people who are trying to kill you, you can no longer have a schedule, or a regular address and phone number, or habits, or a fixed point. This forced instability is enormously disturbing. I let the nights drag on, and then I have violent dreams and sleep very poorly. Now I know what early-morning insomnia is all about! And it's then that I'm afraid of going crazy, like I told you. You're exhausted but you're in anguish, with a lump in your throat, you can no longer stand staying in bed, you don't want to be alone. If you have someone next to you who has to go to work in the morning, you don't want to wake him up. So what I do is pick up a book, as a substitute for the dawn, so that I won't be alone. I don't even see the first few pages. After a while, I get into the book, and eventually I go back to sleep. When I wake up, it's ten or eleven o'clock—and I used to be up at six, before ...

It's a funny life. One of the moments when I'm most aware of that is when I return from abroad. I travel under my own name, with my real passport. That's a decision we made in my movement, because we refuse to behave in our country as if we were in the underground abroad. It's risky—even more so since the taking of the Air France Airbus in December 1994,[2] because now we're obliged to take Air Algérie, and it is even easier for the authorities or F.I.S. agents to track us down on this airline. But we accept the risk. What does that mean? First, that I never reserve my seat. Second, that I spend the shortest time possible at the Boumediene Airport in Algiers, where militants are waiting to come and form a protective cordon around me. Third, that as soon as I've gotten through the airport I jump like a thief into a car—never the same car—where I disguise myself so that I won't be recognized at the various roadblocks, and then I take cover. It is out of the question for me to hang about in Algiers and enjoy the sea air ... Now, the first thing that hits you when you arrive in Algiers is the gentle fragrance of that sea air. The sea ... I can't even look at it! I look at it on postcards, and that's enough! Think about it ... to live there, in that sea-bathed crescent, and no longer really be there ...

What reinforces this feeling is that it's more and more difficult to carve out spaces in which I really feel free. Once you are a militant, someone with political responsibilities, your colleagues expect that you'll always be present, even if you're living in hiding. Given that there were eight of us sharing three rooms when my siblings and I were young, and that I was in a boarding school for seven years, I learned all the strategies for preserving a vital space for myself, very casually. But the problem is when you're being watched: when it comes to friends who dedicate themselves to protecting me, I can't, of course, ask them to leave me in peace. Sometimes they are women, but in general they're men. I end up no longer noticing that these are men who are looking at me.

---

2. Three passengers were killed and several wounded in this incident, which began when four G.I.A.* terrorists disguised as policemen hijacked an Air France Airbus at the Algiers airport and demanded the release of Abassi Madani* and Ali Benhadj*. Although French security forces succeeded in killing the terrorists and liberating the plane's remaining passengers when it landed in Marseilles, Air France suspended all operations to and from Algeria from that point on.

They're my guards, that's all. Without them, without their magnificent, constant devotion, I couldn't do anything anymore. The suffering is elsewhere—for example, in the fact that your most natural desires, like wanting to see your mother or other people you love, have to be discussed. All the militants have to debate about it, decide, and then plan my outing, or my return when I'm abroad. You no longer have any privacy, anything that is just yours. You're obliged to talk about everything, when you'd like to keep these last essential things for yourself. Your desires become public.

E.S.: So, given that you're obviously not demoralized, how do you manage?

K.M.: By living! When I see my mother, after having had a good cry on her shoulder, I start to sing—I was in the chorus in high school!—and I start to dance, to ululate. Even when I'm alone, I dance a good deal. I try to act on my impulses, and I succeed: it's an exercise in self-affirmation, a way of thumbing your nose at the habits that can, under these circumstances, be deadly. Because I'm a bit weird, I decided, as a person who was always maniacally neat, to become disorganized: that was one of the greatest challenges I could give myself. Ah, these are terrible exercises! What else? Everywhere I go, I carry with me my famous green teacher's bag, which has become my house, my self, all by itself. Inside, there's my makeup kit, or at least my lipstick. Before, when I was practicing my profession, I didn't wear makeup. I'd take a shower and be out the door! But since the fundamentalists condemned me to this life, and because they forbid women to wear lipstick and eye makeup, I've taken great care to wear it, every day. It's one of my ways of telling them to fuck off. For me, it is absolutely out of the question to quit—even less so when I'm shut up in an apartment. After I get up, I take my tea, and I begin to get ready, with infinite care, which is the opposite of what I do in normal times; I can spend hours at it. I've learned to savor the pleasure of the Nivea cream that I bring back from Paris and use in frightful quantities. I make it a point of honor to be very neat in my appearance, to be well dressed, to present myself correctly to those who will see me—that is, my guards or the people who come to visit. Standing tall is the most important thing. I have to stand tall at every instant, for myself, and for those whom it inspires. Standing tall.

E.S.: And what if you were kidnapped?

K.M.: You can imagine that I've often thought about that possibility. I'm quite clear-headed about it. I know that, even though I spend my time in the hardest kind of political confrontation and am not afraid of a fight—at least, I don't think so—I am physically horrified by personal conflict. As long as it is a question of ideas, everything is fine. But as soon as an individual is involved, I'm scared stiff. All of a sudden, I don't know what to do. So, you can just imagine me before the torturers of the F.I.S. with their knives and hatchets! I might be able to find the strength not to scream, but I'm not too sure about that. So I'd really like to have a grenade on me at all times, to blow myself up, and them along with me. But the other leaders of the movement won't hear of it. To tell you the truth, I don't dwell on that. When you've had a brush with death, you only think about life afterward. Ever since I received the communiqué from the armed branch of the F.I.S., I've called every minute, every day, every week, every month I've lived "quite beneficial." How long will it have been, tomorrow? Two years. And believe me, the "quite beneficial" year is a lot longer than a normal year!

Chapter 2
The Islam of My Youth

Elisabeth Schemla: Having been born in 1958, you're the same age as your country, give or take four years. You grew up at the same time as it did, and independence was a natural fact for you. You belong, therefore, to the first generation of young Algerians who associated their destiny with the Algeria of the post–war-of-liberation era. What are the consequences of that?

Khalida Messaoudi: They are enormous. First of all, we are the direct inheritors of the heroes of the liberation: we are the sons and daughters of Algeria's refound liberty and dignity. As a group, we admire our parents, each of whom managed, in his or her own way, to resist colonial France. Moreover, we knew that we would have to construct Algeria once we had reached adulthood. That was very exciting because, after the great void left by the French, we were going to be the first wave of professionals who would have to make the country work in every area. Everyone was counting on us. Those are two key elements for explaining that my generation—and probably it alone—is a generation that has no complexes, no shame, no fear of the future. To the contrary! What I mean is that we, and I, have no scores to settle with any enemies. For example, France is, in our eyes, a foreign country like any other. It is, of course, a country with which we have had a certain history, but my generation doesn't spend its time defining itself in relation to France. Our victory was not, in our view, a victory against a certain people but rather a victory against a colonial system. That is not the case with those who were in power, and who still are: their ideological references have been Islam, the classical Arabic language*, and the war of liberation, which they have used as capital for imposing an exclusively Arabo-Islamic identity on us.

That will not be the case with the generation that came after mine, either—a generation that is very important demographically, since 70 percent of the twenty-six million Algerians are under thirty years old. They have an enormous identity problem: their parents did not liberate the country and are regarded not as the "vital strength" of the country, but rather as a burden. Algerian schools only give them one point of reference: the version of Islam espoused by uneducated people and charlatans. Their families no longer protect them. On the other hand, a party comes along and tells them: where does your unhappiness come from? From the Other. This party invents for them an enemy against which they can define themselves. And the Other is women, advocates of secularism, artists, foreigners, Christians, Jews ...

If you don't understand the political psychology, the foundations of the individual and collective personality of those who are now between about thirty and fifty years old, I think that you miss the stakes that are involved. Take someone like me: I am at the turning point between the old men of the F.L.N.*, who have been systematically bleeding Algeria for nearly thirty-five years, and the almost illiterate younger generation, who have no jobs and no housing and who are fascinated by fundamentalism. I don't want either of the visions of society they espouse, and I have been fighting since 1979 for a different model. That model, in its broad lines, is shared by my entire generation, even if we are not all involved in political resistance. Taken as a group, we represent a very large part of civil society, thanks to which our country is still functioning despite the violence. The deep tragedy is that we're being assassinated one after the other, and that everyone acts as if we didn't exist, as if the project for a secular democracy in Algeria was the only one that merited neither respect nor encouragement. The real scandal, it seems, is us. It's enough to make you want to scream—or to want, sometimes, to rise up in arms!

E.S.: Let's get back to you and your personal history. First of all, let's talk about the Islam that your family practiced, from the time of independence up to the present day.

K.M.: I was born in Aïn-Bessem, a typical colonial village one hundred and fifty kilometers from Algiers. But my native village is a village in Kabylia*. It is located about twenty kilometers from Tizi-Ouzou. It is called Sidi-Ali-Moussa, a *marabout** village that has a *zaouïa**, and my family, the Toumis—from the surname the French imposed on us in the nineteenth century—is the marabout family that reigns in the village. I am myself a marabout. E.S.: Before going any farther, could you explain what that's all about?

K.M.: I'll have to go all the way back to the eighth century, to the period when Muslims first entered Kabylia to convert the Berbers to Islam. Among them was Sidi Ahmed ben Youssef, who settled in my village and founded an institution there, the zaouïa, where he preached the word of God and his Prophet, Mohammed, to the villagers. He had no children, but he did have several disciples, including Sidi Ali Moussa, whom he adopted and from whom I am directly descended. When Sidi Ahmed ben Youssef died they built a mausoleum in his memory, and my ancestor enlarged the zaouïa, transforming it into a renowned institute where all the Muslims of the Maghreb came to study. Students boarded there and obtained a diploma. When Sidi Ali Moussa died in turn, the village constructed another mausoleum in his name. Since then the tombs of the two wise men have been places of pilgrimage. These men are venerated there, and people come to make them offerings of money, jewels, and sheep, so that they will intercede with Allah on their behalf during times of misfortune or to have a wish granted. I adore these joyful ceremonies, where women, who are shut inside their entire lives and reduced to eternal silence, can come and unwind for a few hours. All night long, they play the tam-tam drums, and they dance, dance, dance. It's almost like an exorcism, but it harms no one. We are at the heart of this brotherly, typically Algerian brand of Islam*, which can be found in all regions of the country: it constitutes our true religious personality. The movement of fundamentalist *ouléma** had already begun to fight it in 1936, and the F.L.N. continued to do so, but today it is the fundamentalists who have come to despise this form of Islam and want to eradicate it, on the pretext of "returning to the basics." What return to the basics? That makes me laugh! The basics are this brand of Islam, the homegrown kind.

To get back to the zaouïa, it wasn't just a place for religious instruction where one learned the Koran (the word of God), the *hadiths** (the words of the Prophet), and the *fiqh* (the task of interpretation and exegesis of the great ouléma from whom the zaouïa drew its inspiration). One also learned geography and Arabic language and literature there. Moreover, these local institutions, which so clearly reflected the type of social organization that is characteristic of the Maghreb as opposed to the Middle East, were led by a marabout, who also dictated common law and jurisprudence, performed marriages, and resolved disputes over inheritance without being bothered in the least by the central government. Indeed, if there is a region where Islam had to adapt to local customs, it is Kabylia. This situation went on for centuries, up to the Boumediene* era. He sought to put an end, or almost, to this local power, by placing the zaouïas under the control of the Ministry of Religious Affairs—that is, the state. One of his motives, apart from wanting to "break" the popular structures, was that a number of zaouïas had incontestably collaborated with the French colonial system. Mine did not, in any case: it served as a hiding place for the preparation of the November 1 insurrection, and continued to do so during the war years, as Ali Zamoum, one of the heroes of the liberation, recounts in his book *The Country of Free Men.*

E.S.: So you know the Koran, then ...

K.M.: And how! I grew up with the Koran nearby, and I studied it from cover to cover. We had a very beautiful, entirely handwritten copy that had been handed down by my grandfather. When I was little, my father would explain to us that in well-bred families the Holy Book had to be written by hand. In Aïn-Bessem, where we lived in a small house that had been abandoned by some French people in 1962, it was kept inside the sideboard. We studied the family Koran, but we didn't have the right to touch it until we'd reached a certain age. After that, only those of us who knew how to read perfectly and had good diction had access to it. But even then we had to ask permission. My father would make us undergo an interrogation: "Khalida, have you washed your hands?" "Yes." "Good, but did you lie today?" "Yes." "Well then, you're not going to touch it!" And my illiterate grandmother would perform my father's duties perfectly when he wasn't there. In short, having access to this Koran was an honor that we had to deserve, and we were all anxious to do so. I've told that story because, during the big demonstration of civil disobedience that was organized by the F.I.S.* in 1991, I was terribly shocked to see kids parading in the street with this sacred text in their hands and putting it down on the sidewalk. For me, that was an impious gesture.

E.S.: One day, without warning, your father stopped going to the mosque, and you were very impressed. Why did he make that decision?

K.M.: Because he refused to have his way of practicing religion managed or decided by the F.L.N. government, the state. That is what had just happened because of the creation of a Ministry of Religious Affairs, which placed the mosques and imams under its control. In matters of religion, my father has always had two principles that have had a profound influence on me. First, anything ostentatious is detestable. He loathes shouting, ululations, and weeping women. He once told me something that I have never forgotten: "Khalida, when one is a Muslim woman, one doesn't need to advertise it on one's face. You should beware of people who do that—they have a problem." Second, every person is responsible for himself, and himself alone, before God.

I was six or seven years old at the time. I will always remember that Friday. As he did every week, my father put on his *sarouel*—those big, long, heavily pleated pants—along with his vest and his leather shoes, and put his fez on his head. And then he left for the mosque where our imam officiated, an imam who met all the criteria of *charia**: he was married, he had a job (for nobody wanted a lazy imam), and he was an older man who had led a prudent life. That day, however, instead of coming back an hour later as he usually did, my father came home ten minutes later. He's a man who doesn't talk much, and he didn't say a word. But after that incident, I never saw him go back to the mosque. It was only much later that he answered my questions. "What happened? When I arrived at the mosque, I saw that our old imam had disappeared. The Ministry of Religious Affairs had named one whom it liked better—a shepherd, a horse dealer, an ignoramus who feared neither God nor man. You know, my daughter, when you give religion to that kind of person, one day or another it backfires on everyone. I couldn't pray behind this man. I made a decision in my soul and my conscience ..." I gathered from this that it was best to respect the privacy of belief.

E.S.: You said a while ago that the Islam of your childhood was joyful. Was it so different from the kind that is practiced today?

K.M.: Oh, yes! Especially for women! They are the ones who carry on the tradition in a human, sensual way, quite simply because they cook for religious holidays and make them moments of great gaiety. For me, the best example of the difference between the old days and today is Ramadan. My grandmother used to speak about Ramadan with me as if it were a man: "Sidi Ramdan is going to come and stay for a month. So we have to clean the house well, decorate it for him, get out the casserole, and make the stock for the *chorba**." For a long time I thought that Ramadan was, indeed, a man, and I would ask: "When will Sidi Ramdan be here?" My grandmother would also tell me that if everything was really tidy, the *houris*—the eternal virgins of paradise—would be happy. Later, when I went to high school, where I should have fasted (in Islam, girls are obliged to fast during Ramadan as soon as they reach puberty), she exempted me from doing so. She, who had never gone to school, told me that, in God's eyes, when you're studying, Ramadan consists in your studies. And my favorite imam would exonerate me for this! This was, of course, a somewhat pagan Islam, but it was so sincere and pious. When I compare it to these Ramadans that the fundamentalists suggest for us, it makes my hair stand on end! Their version of Ramadan is mortifying. They assume the right to exercise an unlimited control over the observance of religious precepts as they interpret them. There are no songs, no candles, no dances, no Sidi Ramdan or houris. Before the 1991 elections, F.I.S. militias banned all spectacles during the month of Ramadan and barged into cafés in the middle of Algiers, throwing out any customers who were playing dominoes. No Algerians dare to eat in public any more for fear of reprisals. Everything has to be somber. What was a celebration is now a punishment, and what gave spice to life is now a sin. Certain Islamists in the F.I.S. have even banned *Mouloud*, which commemorates the birthday of the Prophet. They view it as a *bidaa*, a heretical innovation of Algerian Islam. The Prophet, they say, was not born Muslim, so we don't have to celebrate that birthday. With them, everything is bidaa. With these crazy people, if my grandmother came back from her grave, she would be assassinated for inciting others to debauchery. Moreover, since February-March 1994, the month of Ramadan has become the bloodiest of the year. First there was the murder of, among others, Katia Bengana, a seven-

teen-year-old high school student, who was killed because she refused to wear a *hidjab** despite the warnings of the G.I.A.* Then
there was the murder of my friend Ahmed Asselah, director of the
Fine Arts Institute, and of his only son, Rabah, right inside the
school. With the car bomb attack that occurred in Algeria last February, the G.I.A. has transformed Ramadan into a month of horror.

E.S.: In your immediate family, who has made the pilgrimage to
Mecca?

K.M.: No one, except for my maternal grandmother ... who went
there three times! The holy place, as you can imagine, is deeply respected—but not the royal Saudi family that acts as its guardian. I
was raised to disdain that caste and was always told that it was
proslavery and corrupt. Morally corrupt, especially. From my earli-
est youth, I was taught in my home that this government was one
of the most unjust on earth; I heard about thieves having their
hands cut off and adulterous women being whipped. I was told
that these unscrupulous people—not the Saudi people, but their
leaders—had barbarous mores and treated women and children
shamefully. Nobody told me exactly what they did to children. I
figured out on my own, afterward, that it involved sexual abuse.
Later, my readings and the testimony of Middle Eastern friends
who had lived there a long while confirmed my suspicions about
what goes on in Saudi Arabia and the countries of the Persian
Gulf.

E.S.: When did you really start to ponder over questions of faith
and religion?

K.M.: During adolescence, of course, when I was in the ninth
grade. Don't forget that I'm a math specialist. I was, and I remain,
a fanatic about the rational method. I would ask myself the classic
questions on the existence of God, but every time I tried to
demonstrate it through logical reasoning, it would be a failure! I
couldn't find a way to touch God, to feel him through intellectual
knowledge. And then I would ponder the concrete consequences
of faith and of Muslim customs.

E.S.: What, for example?

K.M.: For example, I wanted to know what all the sheep killed
for the holiday of Aïd* represented as a loss to Algeria's livestock.
Or the pilgrimage to Mecca: I got the idea of calculating what Al-

gerian pilgrims spent altogether, every year, to go there. I realized that this represented so many municipal libraries, so many movie theaters that wouldn't be built. And I would share my conclusions with my math teacher, to talk about them. I didn't know where this was all going. And then it led, in the tenth grade, to a spiritual crisis.

E.S.: What triggered it?

K.M.: The shock caused by the death of my grandmother, which my parents hid from me to spare me pain. Since my favorite imam wasn't there anymore, he had to be somewhere. So I told myself: "This force that took her and that is helping me to overcome my pain, which I don't know and can't explain, that's God." I adopted this definition once and for all, and I've lived with it ever since.

E.S.: So, contrary to what the Islamists claim about you, you're not an atheist?

K.M.: For them, anyone who is not fundamentalist is an atheist. That is typical of a totalitarian religious vision, and it's for that reason that, contrary to an idea that is still quite widespread, the overwhelming majority of the victims of political Islam are believers. No, I am not an atheist. In a way, I am a deist, but my God has nothing in common with the God of the F.I.S. cutthroats and rapists.

E.S.: On the strength of this definitive conviction, you became a practicing Muslim in the high school where you were a boarder ...

K.M.: I bought a Koran that I read in the dormitory by the light of a pocket flashlight, and a small rug. Out of the sight of the others, I would do my prayers turned toward Mecca, as my grandmother did, morning and night. It was rare to see a young person doing that in Algeria. Prayer, in my day, was for old people.

E.S.: Why didn't you pray five times a day, as one is supposed to?

K.M.: But one is not at all supposed to do that! I dare anyone to find a single verse in the Koran that indicates the number and hour of daily prayers. That's a load of old rubbish! And, in any event, I couldn't exactly interrupt my classes several times a day to leave the room, could I? I would never have accepted that, and I don't accept it today, either. But that is what is happening all over Algeria, and I was faced with it when I was a teacher. Because I had gone through the same thing myself, I understood my students quite well. But I never tolerated having one of them prostrate herself in the middle of a math class. I set the rules of the game, but I always did it by talking to the student in question and using a logical argument: "Miss, I respect your decision, because I, too, prayed when I was your age. But it is out of the question for you not to respect my course. If you choose to leave the classroom, you will not be allowed back in until the next teacher's class." I never had a teenager who preferred prayers over education, in the end. What's more, Islam allows its followers to make up later any prayers they have missed for reasons of work. It's true, however, that the fundamentalist movement was just starting during the time when this was happening, and these students were still very isolated.

E.S.: So, you were seventeen and you were praying ...

K.M.: And one day, I began to be troubled by the position of the believer in Muslim prayer. I'll tell you why ... It was undoubtedly because I am a woman. I found it humiliating to prostrate myself with my head on the ground. I started searching in the Koran to determine which directives required this, and I found nothing. I said to myself: "I have a great and beautiful idea of God. I don't see why I should reduce that idea by adopting a slave position invented by the pro-slavery Bedouins of Saudi Arabia. For us, God is different." And I decided to do my prayers differently from Muslims. My way resembled yoga, so that's how I prayed. One time, my father found me in this position. I explained to him what I was doing. He warned me: "You're not respecting tradition. You're even deviating from it. You should know that you're going to have problems with other people, because the prostrate position you question has been adopted by Muslims all over the world. For them, you're not praying when you're in that position." "But what about for God?" "For God, yes, but you'll have problems." I continued, even so, until two months before the baccalauréat exam. Then I saw the most nonbelieving girls start praying to succeed on their exams. In my eyes, that was an attempt to corrupt God. It was 1977 at the time. I took stock of everything I had observed and lived concerning faith and religion. I put my rug away in a basket and declared that I was finished with all this playacting and hypocrisy, and that I would settle for my personal idea of God. I had definitively become a secular Muslim. And nobody, nobody, should ever bother me again on that subject!

Chapter 3
The Women of the "Deep Interior"

Elisabeth Schemla: The world of women ... let's talk about it, as you observed and experienced it while you were growing up, and as it led you to embrace militant feminism quite quickly when you were twenty-one. Is it even more closed and rigorous in Kabyle* culture than in the others, even though this culture is generally believed to be more democratic, more open?

Khalida Messaoudi: The "openness" of the Kabyle culture is a myth, and people should stop throwing the term around so loosely. Personally, I stake a claim to my Berber heritage, my language, my heroes and heroines, my cuisine, my singers, my poets, because my Algerian personality is also grounded in these Kabyle roots. To renounce those roots would be a kind of self-mutilation. I see it instead as a source of supplementary—but not unique—richness, and I embrace the Berber cultural movement with all my heart. But ... and there is a "but," because I believe too strongly in the universal, in the role of a strong state, in the republican model France handed down to us, to accept a regionalism that defines itself "against" other regions or groups, even if the vast majority of Kabylia is today an outpost of resistance against the authorities and against fundamentalism, which clouds the issue. Given that we'll undoubtedly talk about all that later, I'll get back to the women in my world.

I'd like to show you just how different the situation in Kabylia was from what people imagine. I told you earlier that Islam*, in our culture, was obliged to defer to common law. Well, that law could be more obscurantist than the Koran, which, if it had been applied, would have represented some slight progress. I'll take the most flagrant example of what I call Berber fundamentalism: the example of inheritance. In Kabyle customary law, women have no right to inheritance. None, except in the case where the deceased man had only daughters: then he could write a will that would make them inheritors. Well, do you know when that changed? In 1984, with the Family Code* which was passed by the F.L.N.* parliament and which I am still fighting with all my might. Because it applied to the entire national territory, on this particular point of inheritance, it allowed Kabylia to modify successions just a bit in favor of women ...

E.S.: Are there other examples of this Kabyle uniqueness?

K.M.: The status of widows. Among the Kabyles, if a widow wants to continue to be protected by her family, she must either accept marriage to the brother of her late husband or, if she refuses this remarriage, hand her children over to their father's clan. This is a frightfully hard law for women: given that these women have no other means of supporting themselves, and no education, they are forced to give in. I have an extraordinary maternal grandmother. When she was thirty years old, she found herself alone with her seven children but didn't want to submit to a woman's classic destiny in such a situation. So she confronted her mother-in-law—my Toumi tribe, what a prize!—and insisted that her children were going to stay with her in Algiers, in the Casbah. Just imagine the scandal! She had never worked before; she started to work as a cleaning lady for French families (this was still during the era of colonialism), and her sister joined her with her husband and looked after her kids. She raised all of them to perfection, like a real head of the family. She never again went through any male in deciding how to educate her children, and she has an authority equal to that of a man in the clan. I have enormous admiration for her.

E.S.: What was your mother's lot in life?

K.M.: In her day all women were illiterate. Colonial France did not give Algerian children the right to a normal education, and in our own, patriarchal culture, no one really saw any interest in educating girls. My mother was thus relatively lucky to live in Algiers because she at least went to the "school for natives" up until the fifth grade. She learned how to read, write, and count there, but above all how to sew and iron! When she neared puberty toward the age of ten, her parents took her out of this school to prepare her to become a perfect wife. That was the only future for girls: getting married and having children. Their virginity was carefully preserved, and as soon as they had their first period they were taken to the family of their future husband and the marriage was consummated. For my mother, that happened when she was fifteen, and that was great progress, I dare say, in relation to my maternal grandmother, who I've been told was broken in at the age of nine! Of course, marriages took place only between cousins, to preserve the clan. There is a proverb that says: "If you want the object to be solid, mold it out of your own clay." Or, more rarely, marriages occurred between two clans of equal power. It's true that the familial group takes care of a girl: she is born, and it feeds and raises her, but with the sole purpose of serving the clan of her future husband, of course. I've always had the impression that it's like a programmed history from which no one can escape. My mother therefore married one of her cousins without knowing him in advance—someone whom she had never seen, and who took her from among several female cousins without knowing which one had been chosen for him. Love didn't exist, unless some happy stroke of luck was involved. My parents nonetheless ended up loving each other, and are very close ...

E.S.: Did you mother live more or less confined to the home?

K.M.: In Aïn-Bessem, the village where we lived, my mother did not leave the house.

E.S.: Never?

K.M.: Not once, in more than thirty years. Thirty years without seeing the street. All she knew of the sky was what shone through the open square in the ceiling to the house's inside courtyard. And she, of course, did everything around the house. My mother would have been incapable of describing Aïn-Bessem to you—that is, until the day after I'd gotten married, when I forced her to go to the bath by herself, for the first time.

E.S.: You mean to say that, even for that, she had to be accompanied?

K.M.: It's worse than you think. When I was little, I never went to the bath with my mother. She would only go with the women from two other families with whom we were friendly, after sundown. The three masters, their husbands, would rent the place at great cost for the entire night, because it was unthinkable that their wives be seen in broad daylight.

E.S.: When she went to Kabylia, was she perhaps more free?

K.M.: She didn't go out there, either. Don't forget that she was a *marabout**, a woman of noble caste, and that marabout families are the most atrocious for women. These castes don't tolerate their women working inside the house, except to cook. The rest, all the rest—going to fetch wood or water from the fountain, doing the shopping, cleaning—is done for them by non-marabout women. So my mother never stuck her nose outside in Kabylia, either; she was deprived of all contact with the exterior world by virtue of her "privileges." By contrast, other Kabyle women, non-marabouts, walked around the village wearing the traditional garb, a dress and a *fota**, with a scarf on their heads and their faces uncovered. When I was little, I thought that they were luckier.

E.S.: Didn't your mother ever rebel?

K.M.: No, because she didn't have the choice, and she really loved my father. Inside the house, she ran everything with intelligence and wisdom. And she was a very effective lightning rod for her children when they ran up against the other women in the family, who always wanted rather maliciously to stick their noses into other people's business. My mother exercised her freedom by treating her sons and daughters as more important than the clan, which is unusual. In a society where women keep quiet or only echo their husbands' wishes, she spoke out for herself and for us.

E.S.: Let's get back to the Kabyle village. You mentioned that there were women whose lot in life seemed more desirable than that of your mother. Was it really?

K.M., Oh, no! The fact that these women don't wear a veil does not at all mean that they enjoy equality. I'll say it one more time: there isn't any equality. Let me explain. In our mountain villages, these women work, and they lead a hard life. They can't wear a long robe that impedes their movements. If they have jewelry on their ankles, it isn't to be pretty but to protect that naked part of their bodies from the gaze of men. They don't wear a veil because in the village—as is true everywhere in rural Algeria—the notion of the "outside" world doesn't exist. One is at home, one is inside. This inside is itself divided into two parts, in that there is a tacit sexual division of space: certain routes are reserved for women, and no man has the right to walk there when they are passing through. Thus the first outside gaze, that of the opposite sex, is prevented. Even the mosque, the place of prayer and faith, is off limits to women, because it is situated outside. And when a stranger arrives he is immediately taken in hand by the men. So why would the women wear veils? To get back to my mother and the women in my family, I call them the women of "the deep interior."

E.S.: In the clan system you're describing, virginity plays a major role. You were raised in that perspective ...

K.M.: Yes, of course, and by women! Men—whose whole sense of honor is lodged in that little membrane, the hymen of their daughter or sister—don't handle this part of a girl's education. It is grandmothers and mothers who are the virginity police, the ones who enforce the patriarchal system that oppresses them. They can be formidable toward daughters who have "erred" before marriage. I have awful childhood memories. Not far from Aïn-Bessem, I saw women whose in-laws sent them back the day after their wedding night, because they weren't virgins. They had their heads shaved to mark them with the sign of their infamy, and they were put on a cart and driven through the village. I didn't understand why people did these terrible things. My grandmother would tell me: "Those are barbarians, in our family we don't do that." Later she told me that our old women always had a rooster or a chicken tucked under their arm for a marriage. If the bride wasn't a virgin any more, the women would kill the animal, spread its blood on the sheets, and exhibit it triumphantly. It was imperative to save appearances and honor—but, above all, to protect the clan and the alliances that had been arranged. That was primordial. It was so primordial that everyone pretended to swallow what is called the belief of "the sleeping child." Suppose that, while her husband is away for a prolonged period, a women brings a baby into the world. What's the explanation? She was indeed impregnated by the husband, but the child went to sleep in her womb and didn't develop until awakening several months or years later. Isn't that a great story? I am more or less convinced that if my father had been involved, he would have preferred to accept such a fiction than to break up his tribe! We should note, however, that this is a roundabout way of recognizing women's desire and sexuality. Paradoxically, then, marabout families offer an advantage:

they don't abandon women who have sinned, because the price to be paid—the breakup of the clan—would be too high. For the same reason, such families don't practice polygamy. A great-uncle of mine was the only one to dare to do that, after he had left the village.

E.S.: Did your mother warn you about seduction outside of marriage?

K.M.: The principal role in such matters is played by the father's mother. My grandmother warned me, through veiled language, about marrying beneath my station. It began with that, and started very early. Next, there were rites in which I took part without really knowing what they were all about. I remember one that was done when women were making a *burnous**. The loom consisted of two wooden posts driven into the ground. A boy had the job of passing the thread through to weave the woof, and each time the thread was sticking out, I was supposed to straddle it while pronouncing this formula: "You're a boy, and I'm a wall." This amused me and didn't traumatize me, because I didn't understand much about the symbolism. All the same, it leaves a mark. In fact, people insinuate a great deal around girls until they reach puberty, but it's not until you have your first period that they warn you about illicit pregnancy and seduction. And they do it by telling you impossible things. For example, when you go to take a bath, they tell you to scrub the place where you'll be sitting very well so that you don't get pregnant, because men might have sat there. They tell you that the odor or breath exchanged between male and female cousins can make you pregnant. And they give you a list of all the things you'll be forbidden to do from now on. I thought this was unfair, and I said so: "What do you mean? You've told me that I'm becoming a woman—a responsible grownup—and now you're saying that I don't have the right to do anything?" A council of the women of the family gathered: they told me that Satan can play terrible tricks. I found the story of getting pregnant through breath particularly intriguing. I had learned about how reproduction occurs in mice, and I didn't see why it would be different in humans. So, with an older male cousin—a "scientist" like me—I tried a breath experiment. Wouldn't you know that my aunt walked in at that very moment! It was a minor incident, but a huge business in the family ...

E.S.: You were speaking earlier about the "inside," about the sexual division of space in villages. Was there any contact between the sexes for you?

K.M.: Yes, in the sense that there were four brothers and four sisters in my family. There was also some contact in my larger family, because we saw our cousins a good deal, even if rules intervened after a certain moment. But that was a small pocket of contact, one that was permitted only on the inside. Outside, there was no contact. My high school was exclusively for girls, and I boarded there, so I left it only on weekends to go back to my tribe, but that neither shocked me nor seemed like a burden. As for the street, the Algerian street, I've never had the impression that the sexes mingle there. As far back as I can remember, the women I've seen there have moved quickly from one point to another. In Algerian streets, women don't saunter, they don't stroll—they just pass through.

E.S.: You yourself recognize that the absence of coeducation in your high school did not bother you. So why are you indignant today in the face of the efforts made by the F.I.S.* to impose single-sex education?

K.M.: First of all, at the time, coeducation was the rule in high schools. Mine was an exception, and I accepted it because that was the guarantee of a high-quality education. Second, the intellectual training I received there was a training in freedom for women—whereas the non-coeducation preached by the F.I.S., and which it will try to impose, is the first step in excluding women from the social world.

E.S.: Let's get back to the street. What experience did you have there, as a teenager?

K.M.: A traumatizing one. I lived surrounded by my family. At home, not only was I was praised to the sky like a princess by my father and encouraged in my studies, but I had absolutely the same rights as my brothers. Symbolically, when there was a watermelon on the table, the sweetest part was shared by the boys and girls, contrary to what goes on in most families, where the males get the best of everything. Never, never was I relegated to the position of a woman who should keep her mouth shut and whose femininity is not deeply respected. It was a very protective cocoon. And when I went out into the street with my female cousins men would harass us constantly. It was hell, an obsession for us! On the bus, you would get pawed. Guys gave themselves the right to do that. When I defended myself, when I raised my voice, they would say, at the very least: "You've got nothing to say! Because a girl from a good family doesn't go out, she isn't out on the street!" One day, a guy tried to hit me. I got off the bus, alerted a cop, and asked him to protect me, but he told me: "Move along, a girl from a good family is home at this hour." For the first time in my life, I understood that I was in a country where the state did not defend my right to live the way I wanted to, and I understood that I had no recourse.

But the real shock, and certainly the pivotal experience, took place around 1977, when we were walking down Michelet-Didouche-Mourad Street (the main street of Algiers) with my female cousins. We ran into some men who planted themselves in front of us, stared at our breasts, and started hurling obscenities at us. They insulted our "monstrous tits" and told us, "You should be breast-feeding in your husbands' houses"! There was an enormous violence in this, of the kind that only women can probably appreciate. I felt dirty, humiliated, violated in the deepest part of myself. I cried a good deal, and even today when I talk about it, it hurts like a slap in the face. My grandmother tried to calm me down by saying: "Those are *mlaktin*, people who've lost their bearings." That's exactly so: a bit later, these men would become fundamentalists, obsessed with the totalitarian will to domesticate women's sexuality absolutely, the better to control society.

E.S.: Many girls who now wear the veil, in Algeria or in French suburbs, explain this choice as a desire to escape from the permanent violence of the streets which you describe, and which can be even worse. They say: "With the scarf, men don't bother us any more; it was unlivable before." That is an argument that has more weight and truth than one imagines. I suppose that you understand it ...

K.M.: I understand everything they are feeling, and I know what they want to escape from. I understand that deep down. But, if you think about this business of breasts, as I did right after the incident, what does it mean exactly? That outside, in the world of men where we barely have the right to make a rapid incursion, it is not normal to have breasts and be out on the street, on their property. We have to eliminate this external sign of difference, because we are outside within view of men. For them, demanding that we wear the *hidjab** follows the same reasoning, taken to its logical extreme. They would like us to submit to this as a sort of pass we have to carry. For us, accepting it in order "to be left alone" amounts to accepting the vision men have of us, and perpetuating their system. It's exactly like what I was telling you earlier, when I said that many women were the guardians of virginity, the accomplices of the men in the clan.

E.S.: Did you, even for a moment, consider wearing a veil?

K.M.: You're joking! The question didn't even come up! Never, never, never! Wear a veil? No, but wait ... I am, and we are, Algerian women who stand for emancipation and independence! We're the women who wanted to pursue their studies, practice a profession, make a living, get married and divorced freely.

E.S.: Would your parents have wanted you to carry on the tradition?

K.M.: My mother wouldn't have wanted me to wear a cloth on my head or face for anything in the world. I think it would have killed her if her daughter, her daughters, had to accept the same lot as she did. What she accepted for herself, and internalized, she knew I was able to refuse, and that was her revenge on destiny! As for my father, who was not a liberal regarding women, he was for his daughters, as we've seen. He wanted all of us to have every available means of fitting into the new society that he saw on the horizon.

My parents' generation implicitly admits that, in the context of the country after liberation, their system no longer fits. They are conscious of the ineluctable dismantling of Algerian society. The type of social organization they knew, and which tried for a long while to resist colonization, falls to pieces under rampant industrialization and urbanization. This organization—which I don't in any way want to reproduce—at least permitted everyone, even women, to find a place. My parents don't want their daughters to be lacking for anything as they try to find their place in the new landscape that is taking shape. They're the last of the Mohicans.

E.S.: When you yourself were a teenager, how did you imagine yourself as a woman? Do you remember what kind of woman you wanted to become?

K.M.: I don't want to spin any yarns. Wait ... I remember one image that must be laden with meaning in the eyes of a psychoanalyst. It's the image of a house, with lots of cushions, an immense rug, and books everywhere, everywhere, everywhere. Sometimes there's a man, who's holding a book, too! But he's not a husband. I never imagined myself married. Not on your life! In real life, when one of my aunts would see me and exclaim, "Oh, my girl has gotten so big, she'll be getting married soon!" it would drive me crazy. I couldn't stand the rituals that took place the night before a wedding, when women undid the symbolic seals; or those aphrodisiac recipes that were supposed to excite the husband and keep him faithful—secrets that are handed down from mother to daughter; or the way of treating you like you're a baby machine devoted to the reproduction of the clan, and of considering a sterile woman like the dregs of society; or the obligation of restricting sensuality and pleasure to marriage alone. No, I didn't want any of that. That's all.

E.S.: Did you have models of women who were radically different from the ones you saw around you?

K.M.: Obviously! There was one of my aunts, who was beautiful, sweet, cultivated, and brilliant. And there was my math professor, Fanny Claire Kechich, the embodiment of a modern, competent woman who was fully integrated into external society. But, above all, there were the legendary women who filled my imagination.

E.S.: Who, for example?

K.M.: Lalla Yamina, a woman from the early part of the century who was recognized as a saint—that goes on in the Maghreb!—and who has her own mausoleum in Kabylia. She refused to marry and rebelled against her family. People told me about her with admiration, for she was a great sage but also someone who had a rifle that she would use when a really flagrant abuse was committed and men didn't correct it. Then there was Lalla Fadhma N'-Soumeur, who, from 1850 to 1855, organized the armed resistance against French colonization in Great Kabylia, as the women of Ouled Sidi Cheikh did elsewhere in Algeria. She was eminently subversive because she conducted her fight from a mosque, and did so for ten years! She was arrested by a French general and ended her life in prison. Finally, there was la Kahina, a Judeo-Berber queen from the Aurès* mountains, a redhead with white skin from the land of the Chaouia*. She is a living myth in all our memories, and no one will ever be able to kill her. I grew up in adoration of her. In our family, when a girl is brave she is told: "You, you're la Kahina!" For years, in the eighth century, she led the army that was resisting the Arab invaders. To avoid giving herself up to the enemy, she killed herself.

E.S.: As a redhead with white skin who joined the resistance, flirted with the idea of taking up arms against the fundamentalists, and considered carrying a grenade to blow yourself up in case you were kidnapped by an F.I.S. commando, don't you, perhaps, see yourself as a warrior, a modern-day Kahina?

K.M.: I try to command respect using my means, which are peaceful: words. If a fundamentalist movement that has weapons and money condemns a woman like me to death, it is because I constitute a danger to its project, and thus I am right in what I am saying against it. So the madmen of God would like me to go back to the basics of submission? I only want to go back to the basics of dignity. La Kahina influences me, deep down; I can't deny that. But you've got to be kidding if you imagine that I am a distant descendant of her! Evoking this woman, and all the other women from Algeria as a whole who have always known how to rise up when they had to, makes things easier for someone who is taking part in the difficult task of creating and leading a women's movement. Times are different, and the causes for resistance are, too, but in all these cases liberty has been at stake. You see, whether we're talking about my personal history or that of my country, I have every reason to refuse to submit to any yoke.

Chapter 4
The Daughter of Voltaire and of Averroës

Elisabeth Schemla: Knowledge and education are at the heart of your life. You're a perfect model of a "prize for excellence" winner, and you won it, moreover, almost every year up to the baccalauréat. I'm not certain that your route would have been the same during the period when Algeria was a French colony. You and I both went to the same school, but a few years apart, and, up to 1962, I don't remember seeing a single Arab or Kabyle* student in that high school. How did the emerging Algerian state help you?

Khalida Messaoudi: Independence had barely been declared when the state made a major political decision: to provide free education. I have been sufficiently critical and vociferous toward this single-party government over the past fifteen years to acknowledge that. At the time, the balance of power within the F.L.N.* between the Islamo-baasist* tendency and what I would call the socialist-modernist tendency leaned toward the latter, and Boumediene* was all-powerful, in all his glory. Thanks to oil revenue and the state of the international petroleum market, he was able to invest in education. I benefited from this revolution, as did all the children who were my age. At the end of primary school, because I was a good student, I won a scholarship to continue my studies at the high school level, in Algiers. Without this help from the government, that wouldn't have been possible, given the rather meager salary my father earned as a civil servant. Probably, only two out of the eight of us children in the family would have been able to pursue our studies. And you have to keep in mind how anxious my parents were for us to do so! They were ready to make all sorts of sacrifices so that we could attend the best schools. That is why my oldest brother was sent to a Catholic boarding school run by priests of the "Pères Blancs" order, three of whom were savagely killed by the F.I.S.* recently in Tizi-Ouzou—another act that horrified me. It is always said that "The Kabyles adore school," as if they were in some way intellectually superior to other people. Superior in what way? It makes me laugh! The truth is, the region is poor and the people are, too, which means that they have very little besides education to pass on to their children. I was steeped in the Kabyle belief that knowledge is sacred, whereas those miserable Islamists hold knowledge in contempt.

E.S.: You just mentioned free education. Wasn't it obligatory?

K.M.: No. And that's another reason that I can't give the F.L.N. unqualified praise, even on the subject of education. I'll go even farther. For example, when a woman friend of mine was taken out of school because she was married, the state didn't intervene. It didn't guarantee her right to be educated. So you see that, right away, the government accepted having patriarchal law, even the law of *charia*, take precedence over any other law.

E.S.: This isn't the first time you've shown a particular concern—an obsession, even—with the state. Why is that?

K.M.: Because my father, a civil servant, had an absolute respect for it, just as he did for education. In the context that has framed my life since childhood, Allah, Mohammed, Jules Ferry*, and the *Code communal* are inextricably tied. They were permanent guests at the table where we gathered every evening to do our homework, around my father, who was himself always working on his paperwork. He had copies of the Code within arm's reach, along with a municipal stamp and its ink bottle. One day, one of my little brothers took that stamp and stamped his notebook in secret. No one had seen him do it. My father had each one of us recite our lessons, and, the moment he sat down in front of my brother, he saw the notebook and the stamp. He flew into an unimaginable cold fury. He examined every sheet, every page of all our notebooks and all our books to check whether we had committed the same infraction. It took forever. Then he sent us to bed without dinner, telling us: "What your brother did was extremely serious, more serious than stealing. He used the state for himself, for his amusement. That is a crime." Believe me, a father's fury and condemnation make an impression on young minds. After the Koran, the *Code communal* was the second sacred thing, and when I dared to touch it, my brothers and sisters would stop me: "You're crazy, you're touching the state! You don't have the right!" My father raised us according to this myth, which he'd inherited from colonial France and which he believed was good for his liberated country. Of course, when you realize later that disrespect for the state originates in the state itself, you're shocked. That is exactly what happened with the F.L.N., and it continues to this day.

E.S.: Your father oversaw your education very closely. What did he insist on?

K.M.: Before we entered primary school, he demanded that each of us know the alphabet in French and the multiplication table. Ah, the table! He focused so much on that ... I think that, in his eyes, math must have been the height of culture.

E.S.: And French was the language of culture?

K.M.: Without a doubt.

E.S.: All this took place barely twenty-five years ago, after one hundred and thirty years of colonial occupation. For the "Muslim French," the colonial period translated, from a linguistic point of view, into a more or less successful coexistence of the two local idioms, the Algerian dialect of Arabic and French, in daily life if not in the schools. After independence, however, languages* became one of Algeria's major problems and stakes. Through them, the very definition of the country's identity was being forged. What did you speak at home?

K.M.: My parents spoke their native tongue, Kabyle, between themselves. That was the language of the inside. Of course, they also spoke Algerian Arabic and French in all the circumstances in their lives where it was necessary. They believed, however, that their children should first speak the language that would allow them to fit in, in the world outside. In the outside world, that language was Algerian Arabic. And at school, French and classical Arabic were spoken. So my father and mother made an effort to address us in Algerian Arabic. Thus, although Kabyle is a part of the world I share with my mother—I sing in Kabyle, for example, because singing is the deepest expression of oneself—Algerian Arabic is my mother tongue.

E.S.: When you entered nursery school, and then primary

school—this was in 1963-64—what were the languages of instruction?

K.M.: I was taught to read and write ... in two foreign languages, classical Arabic and French, simultaneously. I didn't choose between the two. I regarded both as academic languages, different from the one I was using in the street and at home. But I'm more at ease in French than in classical Arabic. In spite of everything, French was a part of Algeria's natural landscape, it was familiar to my ears, and I had skimmed through my big brother's books—the inevitable collections of La Fontaine's *Fables* and Victor Hugo's poems. By contrast, who had ever spoken to me in classical Arabic, when had I heard it, who was reading it? There was no way I could experience it as my language, as the language of Algerians, or as one of the languages of my national history. It's exactly as if you were suddenly to assert that the language of the French is Latin! Classical Arabic was the equivalent, for us, of Latin for the French. Today, when someone in Algeria says he is bilingual, what does that mean? That he speaks classical Arabic and French! How insane! I, for example, maintain that I am quadrilingual, because no one is going to force me to forget that my first languages are Algerian Arabic and Kabyle!

E.S.: Why did the government decide to impose the "foreign language" of classical Arabic on the country's children instead of teaching them Algerian Arabic, and "Arabize" the entire school system?

K.M.: The decision to align the Algerian identity with Arabo-Islamism and to impose classical Arabic as the sole national language of Algerians was made before independence, during the national movement. In 1949, a crisis in the P.P.A.-M.T.L.D.* was resolved in an authoritarian manner by the proponents of Arabo-Islamism. The F.L.N. government that grew out of the national movement was destined to continue that approach and institutionalize the state of affairs. From what does this stem? In essence, it stems from the antidemocratic, Jacobin nature of the F.L.N., which was very, very much afraid of all expressions of popular culture and wanted to impose a "culture" of its own making, using it to crush popular culture in all its manifestations. The leaders of this government also promoted self-hatred to an alarming degree. The only thing that doesn't fit in the equation is the fact that those leaders did everything possible to ensure that their own children were shielded from all this. In fact, I defy anyone to find me one child of an F.L.N. official who had a scholarship anywhere other than in a Western country.

E.S.: At the end of primary school, you got a scholarship that allowed you to go to Algiers. Thanks to your exam results, you enrolled in one of the best schools in Algeria, the former Franco-Muslim high school that had become Hassiba Ben-Bouali High School, and you stayed there until the baccalauréat. In this privileged establishment you would experience first-hand the progressive and catastrophic Arabization of the school system. When did you become aware that a great turning point had occurred?

K.M.: It was in 1971, when, as a sixth-grader, I was automatically placed in the school's first completely Arabic class ... In fact, the Arabization of the secondary school system that Boumediene sought to establish began in 1968. Was it possible for these government idiots to do things rationally by disturbing as little as possible the young people who had already been terribly disrupted by the cultural changes to which they were subjected? No, of course not! The F.L.N. had already decreed, overnight, that a certain number of courses be taught entirely in classical Arabic: history and philosophy in the tenth grade, and philosophy in the senior year. And then the F.L.N. went and made certain classes all-Arabic, just like that. These were experimental classes, and it was soon apparent that only poor children got placed in them. Let's take my high school ... Because it was a top school, the upper crust of the regime enrolled their children there. In our student body there were, among others, the niece of Boumediene and the niece of Taleb Ibrahimi, that good Minister of Education who promoted reform but obviously didn't want it for his family! The all-Arabic class wasn't good for the daughters of the ruling class—who stayed in the sections taught in French—but it was for those of us who were boarders, like me. And it didn't matter what our level was, given that I, for example, was, without boasting, one of the best students in the school.

E.S.: Did you have to deal with those horrendous foreign teachers brought in from Egypt, Syria, and Iraq, who have become so notorious?

K.M.: And how! For me, their nationality was not the problem.

But it is clear that our "big brother" Nasser, for example, did not send us Egypt's best teachers to Arabize our school system. And Ben Bella*, the prime minister, didn't find it useful to pay close attention. I remember one Egyptian math teacher. I don't know what this guy's background was, but he was shameful. He couldn't have cared less about what he was doing and he was grossly incompetent: I swear I knew more math than he did! Outside of Arabic, he didn't speak a single word of French and only a few words of English. So, to describe the "empty set," for example, he would join the Arabic word for "set" with the English adjective "empty." That's what he did for everything. Given that we only had a passing grasp of classical Arabic and were just starting to study English, most of us were lost right away. What's more, almost all my classmates went home on the weekend and, instead of being able to catch up in their studies, had to do housework: they had to pay their dues for getting an education, as in all poor families! In conditions like these, you can get hopelessly behind very fast ... It was the same story in every subject matter. We didn't learn anything and didn't do any work. The school system was tossing us a two-bit culture that had been conceived and carried out for the new "indigenous" population. It was all terribly unfair: you could feel that the system was making knowledge inaccessible to you.

E.S.: How did you cope?

K.M.: I was sad, and completely lost. I had tried in vain to alert the assistant principal, who would take refuge behind the ministerial orders. I was saved by the Arabic teacher: he had taken such a strong dislike to me that he gave me a zero on every exam. It ended up attracting the principal's attention. We also had a Syrian woman on the science faculty who fought for me by saying that, if they left me like that, they'd ruin my life. So there were also some good people among these foreigners. In a word, at the end of the first semester of my seventh-grade year I was put into a "normal" class—that is, a French one that was called "bilingual." Given my familial environment, I was already not very disposed to adore the government, and even though I myself had escaped the worst, I was quite shocked to see how the scholarship students were treated compared to the daughters of wealthy families. I took my revenge later. In the dormitory, I gave catch-up classes to my fellow boarders, so that we would show up the ministers' daughters.

E.S.: Did the government have any solution other than importing these teachers, given that the massive departure of *pieds noirs* [French settlers in or native of Algeria] had completely deprived Algeria of its professionals?

K.M.: If, for the reasons I gave earlier, the F.L.N. had not decided to pursue this hasty and extreme Arabization, and if it had chosen to have classes taught bilingually in Algerian Arabic and French, the drama wouldn't have happened. For one thing, we would all have been working in our natural language, and our teachers would have been, too; for another, Algeria would have attracted a good number of first-rate volunteers from France, I'm sure of it. Despite the difficulties that arose from demography, the education system would have attained a level worthy of a nation that both respected its personality and was integrated into the modern world. But, you see, there was nothing innocent in all this. For, by controlling the language of instruction, the F.L.N. wanted to control the very content of what was taught. The proof is what happened in conjunction with the Arabization of the secondary schools.

The problem was not so much importing teachers from this or that country as knowing what definition of the Algerian nation was desirable. When you see that, today, one young Algerian takes himself to be an Afghan or an Iranian, whereas another dreams only of escaping Algeria through any means possible, it is clear that the policy of the F.L.N. was a real disaster. In the face of this disaster, the F.I.S. asks us to obliterate ourselves by joining the "Muslim nation," whose geographical contours have never been traced; the Algerians who are republican democrats want, by contrast, to save Algeria by bringing forth a model of the citizen whose complex identity would be respected. That identity would include Berber, Arab, and Muslim dimensions, and the idea of belonging both to the Mediterranean region and to Africa. And we shouldn't consider any of these elements as mutually exclusive. I don't think that we would lose our souls by loving what has made us what we are. All we would have to do, after taking that step, is come up with the means of attaining our objective.

E.S.: What are the most surprising decisions that Boumediene made?

K.M.: Well, Boumediene—the socialist-modernist who, as everyone forgets, studied at the fundamentalist Al-Azar University in Cairo—established secondary schools for Koranic studies throughout the country. Under the pretext that it wasn't possible to build middle schools and high schools in every village and that it was imperative to "educate" everyone, he filled the country with these Koranic schools. On the advice of Mouloud Naït Belkacem, a Kabyle Minister of Culture, Boumediene made access to these schools easy for all young people and handed out scholarships in function not of the student's talent but of his or her desire to study the Koran. These schools have nothing to do, however, with *medersas*, the traditional Koranic courses you could take Wednesday afternoons after school. In addition to offering a general education that is drastically reduced in comparison to the secular system, the schools Boumediene established instruct their students in fundamentalism. And, at the end of the course of study, they hand out a diploma that is supposedly equivalent to the baccalauréat! Who is it that trains these young people? The fundamentalist mutants who come to Algeria from all the countries where they're already at work. Here, again, the government doesn't want to adapt this very "specialized" theological instruction to Algerian realities: like a Jacobin in a land that isn't Jacobin (that, unfortunately, is the only model the government has retained from France), its objective is to crush the country's multiple religious identities in order to help establish not a democracy but a dictatorship. The tragedy, you see, is that no one is paying attention to what is being set in place, or sounding the alarm about it. Boumediene himself constructed the first pockets of fundamentalism, which would later serve as the basis for the Islamists' seizing of power, without triggering the slightest warning! The party's repressive system smothered the impulse to revolt. And that wasn't the end of it! During the 1980s the "religious" types also began squatting in the public schools. Then, in the secular high schools, sections devoted to "Islamic science" appeared; these eventually gave rise to a baccalauréat in "Islamic science." I myself witnessed their creation in the schools where I was teaching.

E.S.: It is always somewhat difficult to understand why the F.L.N. government itself produced fundamentalism. How do you explain, for example, the fact that Boumediene initiated this policy?

K.M.: Don't forget that we're talking about a single-party system.

As is always the case in such a situation—except when there are other parties that radically oppose dictatorship, like the party of Mohamed Boudiaf*—all the various ideological currents coexist within the totalitarian structure. In this instance, that structure contained the two major tendencies I mentioned earlier. Partisans of the Islamo-baasist tendency saw the ideology of Islamic pan-Arabism as a model for Algeria, whereas the socialist-modernists believed in liberation through economic and military development. The second camp, which was dominant at the time, was naturally obliged to make a few concessions to the other side in order to keep the peace and snuff out any fratricidal infighting. One of these concessions—the other one was on the subject of women—was to offer the other camp the school system, which wasn't considered a "key sector" for development! Taleb Ibrahimi, who was friendly with Roland Dumas and François Mitterand and who is, oddly enough, seen by many French politicians as an alternative to our current debacle, was one of the artisans of this strategy. He took care to protect his own children from the effects of what he'd done. It's as simple and terrible as that.

E.S.: Let's get back to your studies and to the content of the curriculum you were describing earlier. There are usually certain key areas that illuminate a policy. Did you have, for example, courses in religious instruction?

K.M.: What's interesting is that, in the beginning, we had some courses in pure civics. Then they became courses in civic and religious instruction. Today, they're courses in Islamic education. I think that says a great deal about the underlying intent and evolution of these courses. In my day, they essentially consisted in inculcating some moral principles and practical advice in us. The advice was of this sort: how should a young girl cleanse herself after her period in order to resume fasting or praying? We were also explained the foundations of our religion, like the five pillars of Islam; this was done in classical Arabic. It was the kind of training that one might not think a secular school should provide, but it was a far cry from the terrible brainwashing to which Algerian children would be subjected a bit later, under Chadli*.

E.S.: And what about history?

K.M.: Ah, history! There's a lot to be said about that area. Or rather, there's one major thing to be said: we were taught a history that had been falsified, revised, and corrected by the winners within the F.L.N. and those to whom they had given the "school concession." Even though I was quite young, I was aware of this: the names of the heroes of the national liberation movement that we heard all the time at school and in the textbooks were not the same as those that I heard at home. Here are a few revealing examples: Ben Badis*, who founded the Association of *ouléma** in 1936, had argued for cultural and religious autonomy and pronounced himself opposed to the independence of Algeria during the colonial era. He advocated a fundamentalist Islam like that of the Muslim Brothers, to which he belonged; he was opposed to all the local Muslim practices, which he called *chaouadha*, or charlatanism. In my family, I heard people talk about Ben-badists as fanatical missionaries who saw Algeria as a land of conquest for religious fundamentalism. Compared to the precursors of November 1954, the Ben-badists could even be considered traitors. In the history textbooks we read in high school, however, Ben Badis was being praised to the skies and presented as the father of the country's independence movement! He was thus acquiring a very dangerous legitimacy in the eyes of the new generations! Once again, Boumediene accepted this imposture because it suited his own desire to eradicate the native forms of Islam and native structures of power. By contrast, the great Messali Hadj* was practically erased from the history books, or called a traitor because he had created the M.N.A.* My mother, who was a rebel, was beside herself when I told her about this: "But do they at least tell you about the people who liberated the country, the real heroes of history, like Mohamed Boudiaf, Abane Ramdane, Krim Belkacem, Ouamrane, Ben Bella, and Aït Ahmed*?" I was obliged to say no. And my mother went on: "But this Boumediene, where does he come from, since no one had ever heard of him before or during the war? Don't listen to them!" This was how I learned that the history I was being taught was a history written by the authorities to dumb down the Algerian people and deprive them of their memory; it was a history that only served men who held a totalitarian power.

E.S.: Let's talk for a minute about Aït Ahmed, to whom you are opposed today. What exactly were you told about him?

K.M.: That he was a hero and, to be honest, *the* hero of the Kabyles. He was described to me as a great nationalist, a great patriot who had fought for independence and then had become an anti-establishment figure who had tried to impose his views, after independence. When he came back to Algeria, one day, this exceptional man would change everything—he would be the great hope of the country. My father himself took part in Ahmed's movement, the F.F.S.*, the Socialist Forces Front. He was imprisoned in 1963 as an F.F.S. militant and fund raiser, and he stopped being politically involved when the Front lost the battle. I was raised in the Aït Ahmed myth—and, even more so, in the hope of his return.

E.S.: Up to what point did the war of liberation serve as a grid for interpreting the other events in the history of the world that you were being taught?

K.M.: It was the sole grid. Algeria was a mirror that reflected a single image of the world. The conditioning was so powerful that I was incapable of picturing Pinochet as anything other than a foreign invader from whom Chile had to be liberated through a nationalist war. It wasn't until I'd met refugees from Santiago several years later that I realized, much to my amazement, that Pinochet was himself Chilean! Likewise, we were told that the Israeli-Palestinian conflict was a war of total liberation required to chase out a colonial presence—the Jews—but we were never told anything about the Jews' history, or about the genocide they had suffered, or about the complexity of this business. I learned about that genocide in 1979 during my first stay in France, and I was deeply shaken by it. I've read a good deal about it since then, and I've obviously revised my position on the subject. But, you know, all this represents a series of painful mutations, because the F.L.N. never taught us in Algeria to be free thinkers.

E.S.: I suppose you were not taught about the war of liberation alone ...

K.M.: According to the textbooks, the history of Algeria began with the arrival of the Arabs and Islam. Before that, there was nothing—as if the Berbers, the Phoenicians, the Romans, and others had not existed. As for the Turks and the Ottoman Empire, they were presented not as occupiers but as a "Muslim presence." Only one history teacher, a woman who taught my ninth grade class, told us that, in the form in which she was forced to teach it to us, this material was a fraud. She gave us the references for books that we couldn't find in our country but could get in France, and said: "If you can, read them, read ...!" She was very brave, because, under the dictatorship, she could have been denounced by one of her students. Listen, apart from her, I was lucky to have had my grandmothers, first of all, my aunts, all the old people in the family, and then all the books I was able to consult. For official television simply echoed the distorted history we got in our schoolbooks. The films we could see, which were often Egyptian, sent a single message: Arabo-Muslims are the most attractive, the most intelligent, the most courageous, the most everything; they have never made any mistakes, and wherever they have gone the population has naturally, spontaneously embraced Islam; the Prophet was a really nice guy, and his friends were, too, but all the others who didn't agree with them were villains and bastards who in any case were going to lose. It was, altogether, an unbearable environment. If I had had to rely on the Algerian school system—and state television—to teach me history, I would be a fundamentalist calling for lynchings today!

E.S.: But you were nonetheless lucky as a student at Hassiba Ben-Bouali High School, given that, above and beyond what you've just described, you had access to several cultures ...

K.M.: That's true, and it remained true until 1980. The school choir was one of the strongest remaining expressions of pluralism in privileged schools like mine. We sang *L'Amour de toi* by Ronsard, Negro spirituals, and songs in Algerian, Kabyle, and Andalusian, like the famous *Touchiat es-Sultan*. I had music courses where I became familiar with Beethoven, Mozart, Schubert, and Tchaikovsky. Today, all that has disappeared because it is considered "imported" culture. And for the F.I.S. such works are the work of Satan. During the holidays, we would dance in the costumes of all the regions in Algeria. There were as many different costumes and types of music as there are regions, and they were all Algerian. So who can claim that one costume is more national than another? And what is the legitimacy of the "national Islamic costume" that the fundamentalists want to impose on us?

E.S.: What about philosophy?

K.M.: That was *the* course, taught by a magnificent teacher who was barely thirty years old and an Arabic-speaking communist. His name was Rabah Guenzet. For the first time in all my school years,

I heard the same values, the same culture defended in Arabic as I heard defended in my French-language courses. It was a revelation, because Arabic had up to that point been the language of political propaganda, including in the newspapers—and *El Moudjahid* in French wasn't any better. Guenzet did even more than that: along with having us study European philosophers like Kant, Nietzsche, and Spinoza, whose works we had to read in French of necessity because no translations are available in Algeria, he taught us Arab philosophers using their original texts. It was an exhilarating year.

E.S.: So was he cheating, in relation to the syllabus?

K.M.: He was extremely skilled at bending the official line. He put the age of Enlightenment on the syllabus, and we studied Montesquieu, Diderot, d'Alembert, and Voltaire. He told us about the stakes of the debates between Danton and Robespierre, he delved into the mysteries of the fledgling French Republic, and he explained the role of a national assembly, of a parliament.

Besides that, he had decided to talk with us about two poles of Islam where intellectual ferment had produced exciting works between the eighth and twelfth centuries: the Middle East and Andalusia in Spain. At the very beginning of the school year, he had handed out a text by Averroës, or Ibn Ruchd, an Arab philosopher born in Andalusia during the twelfth century, whose revolutionary work had shown for the first time during the Golden Century the interrelation of philosophy and science and of philosophy and religion, and whose disciples included Jews, Christians, and Muslims. This period of Spanish history, where three cultures and three religions intermingled in the Al-Andaluz kingdom, fascinated him. Guenzet vividly described to us what a free thinker Ibn Ruchd was. He accentuated two points: first, philosophy and religion are not contradictory; and second, to ensure that religion retains its sacred character, one must not confuse it with philosophy, either. He argued, in a word, that to go as far as one can in philosophical reasoning and analysis, one has to know how to keep one's beliefs in check without abandoning them. He stressed how valuable it was, for that purpose, to enrich one's thinking by debating people with radically different perspectives. Averroës had also written an incisive text on the place of women. He showed that any society that subjugates women inevitably falls into decadence. I'm sure you realize what that idea must have represented in his age! I was deeply influenced by it. Guenzet underscored how close Ibn Ruchd was to us, for at the time Andalusia was an extension of our Maghreb, even though it was autonomous.

In addition, Guenzet introduced us to the Mouà Tazilites, a school of thinkers who inspired the Abbasid dynasty in Damascus. It was a period of great intellectual and cultural production, where a peaceful Muslim government was interested in rationality, allowing Muslim thinkers to reflect on Islam, to compare the voice of the Koran to the voice of reason, and to justify the predominance of the latter if its conclusions seemed better. As of the eleventh century, this school was considered by the Abbasids themselves to be an elitist group that was dangerous to faith. Over the course of a century the Mouà Tazilites were assassinated, decimated. What happened in relation to Islam itself? Mohamed Arkoun tells the story brilliantly: after the eleventh century, the doors were shut! That is, Islam's leaders systematized the religion in writing and repressed all efforts at interpretation, according to the will of the caliph. They wrote the Sunna* and dictated the way Muslims should think and act. There was no salvation outside official dogma. As Arkoun puts it, Islam "was henceforth the institution of the unthought in Muslim thought." These are two periods in Muslim history that are never discussed in Algerian schools.

We were flabbergasted. We were living under the regime of the "closed mouth" that the one-party system imposed on us from the outside. And inside the school we were hearing things which had to remain confidential and which were transforming our young minds. We had a philosophy teacher who, all of sudden, was telling us about Arab countries where it had been possible to think, to think about Islam, and to discuss it with other people. And there we were, repeating the same question over and over again: "But, Mr. Guenzet, are you sure that this happened in an Arab country?" Rabah Guenzet would answer yes, he was sure, but that in Damascus as in Andalusia, totalitarians of all sorts—Arabs or Spaniards, Muslims or Christians—had always ruined everything for everyone.

E.S.: You said that Guenzet was a communist. Did he tell you about Marx, Lenin, and Trotsky?

K.M.: No. But he was also our drama teacher, and he introduced us to Brecht, explaining that there was no insurmountable barrier between Brecht and our Algerian theater. He would take *L'Homme aux sandales de caoutchouc* [*The Man in the Rubber Sandals*] by Kateb Yacine*, and he'd try to demonstrate that Brecht and Yacine were from the same school of theater. So, what was my dream, thanks to Guenzet? To meet Kateb Yacine in the flesh, an author who was cursed and denigrated by the F.L.N. because he was free, anti-establishment, wrote in French and did theater in Algerian Arabic. I don't have to tell you how moved I was when Kateb came to give a lecture at my university a few years later.

Of course I had already read and studied *Nedjma*, without really understanding it. I heard this man speak to us in exceptional French and declare: "French is one of the spoils of our war." For the first time, I began to think about French, but more as the language that provided access to texts of literature and philosophy. I pondered its status in Algeria. I realized that Kateb—like Mouloud Mammeri or Mohamed Dib and others—had used it as a weapon against the colonial system, as a weapon of conceptualization. As soon as I realized that, I not only found it more natural to speak French, I also told myself: "This is great, I'm appropriating this language as an instrument. I'll never let go of that." You see, it is for this Algeria that I am fighting, an Algeria where it is possible to be a Berber speaker, a French speaker, and an Arabic speaker, all at once, and to defend the best of all three cultures. Guenzet's message lay in that truth, and it has been permanently stored in my memory.

E.S.: Did Voltaire and Averroës prolong their stay in your high school?

K.M.: Obviously not! Both of them were soon eliminated, Averroës along with Voltaire, even though he was an Arab or perhaps because he was an Arab who thought modern thoughts. But I am the daughter of both thinkers, and I remain so.

E.S.: What happened to your mentor, Rabah Guenzet?

K.M.: I ran into him again when I was a university student, and he became my friend ... For a long time, we diverged in our analyses of the political situation and disagreed on the best strategy to adopt, but we did this precisely in the spirit of what he had taught me so well. Then, one day, we ended up in total agreement, unanimous in our actions. Then Rabah was fatally shot in the head by the F.I.S., in 1994.

E.S.: ...

K.M.: ...

E.S: I imagine Rabah Guenzet wasn't the only communist teacher you had. Did the others also make an impression on you?

K.M.: I owe a lot to my other communist teachers, my French teacher and my history teacher. They provided an education based on thinking, and they talked about justice and liberty, and I must have had some sort of predisposition for listening to them on those subjects. You have to remember that my father was a liberal. He never agreed to carry an F.L.N. card, despite the pressure to do so. Throughout my childhood, I saw him talking about the rights of citizens, devising communal development plans to help young people, and lending a hand to everyone. I also saw him, one day when Boumediene was making an official visit to Aïn-Bessem, be the only person in the village to stay home very conspicuously, in order to demonstrate his rock-solid disapproval in a silent way. In a word, I was unconsciously liberal, and I affirmed my left-leaning inclinations beginning in the tenth grade, thanks to all these teachers we've just discussed, who were enjoying their last moments of freedom.

E.S.: Was there really an Islamic infiltration already occurring in "normal" sections when you were a student?

K.M.: Today, I can say yes, but it would be false to claim that I had, at the time, attached words of that sort to the incident I'm about to recount. It shows this infiltration quite well. It was in 1977 ... Yes, as early as that ... I was in my senior year. In another philosophy class, the woman who was teaching the subject had told her students about the virtues of an Islamic state that had existed long, long ago. An Islamic state? ... This became a point of heated discussion in the courtyard between the girls in her class and us, who had Guenzet as a teacher. So Guenzet suggested that the students of the two classes organize a debate on this state. And so we did. During this debate, one of the students on our side asked the other teacher very politely to describe the political and economic system of the state in question, the relation between the leaders and the governed, and those of the governed among themselves. The woman could only find one example, that of Saudi Arabia! Thanks to her parents, undoubtedly, the student was quite knowledgeable about that country. She began to tell everyone about the *bidouns*, something the rest of us had never heard of.

E.S.: Who are the bidouns?

K.M.: These are, in the strict sense of the term, "people without a name." They are people who counted for nothing, whose lives had no value in a slave system. They're people whom nobody has kept track of, because of the Saudi monarchy, which blithely defies international laws. In short, for us girls, this Islamic state based on the Saudi model was shameful, unacceptable. It was at that point that the woman teacher flew off the handle and said to Guenzet: "These aren't students you have, they're hoodlums!" It's clear, in hindsight, that this woman was linked to the movement of Muslim Brothers.

E.S: In 1977, you were nineteen years old and you passed the baccalauréat. You were getting ready to go to university. One year later, Boumediene would be dead. Did you more or less sense the upheaval that was coming?

K.M.: Not in the least, despite the presence of the warning signs I've told you about. That's because it was impossible, at the time, to decode their general meaning. Like many adolescents of my generation, I thought my future would lie in the difficult but certain triumph of democracy.

Chapter 5
Code of the Family, Code of Infamy

Elisabeth Schemla: As you were emerging from adolescence, Chadli Ben Djedid*—yet another military leader!—came to power. For you, a precocious militant at the University of Algiers, it was a time of fundamental political choices. You wouldn't swerve from those choices thereafter. They would lead you to fight the new leader of the all-powerful F.L.N.* without reserve, right up to the fall of Chadli and of the party in 1991. I should add that, as a woman, a student, and then a teacher who was bilingual but chose to teach in French, a republican and a secularist, you were at the heart of the fundamentalist turmoil that Chadli provoked. You were a living example of the kind of Algerian woman that the ruling party sought to eradicate, using all the means at its disposal ...

Khalida Messaoudi: I'm glad to hear you use the term "eradicate" in speaking of the F.L.N.! That's because today I'm the one who is called an "eradicator" for trying to speak out and prevent the F.I.S.*—which the F.L.N. itself produced—from assuming power, and for opposing any negotiations with the fundamentalists.

E.S.: I use the term intentionally, Khalida, to underscore the extreme violence, renewed from generation to generation, that has wracked Algeria—an Algeria whose sons and daughters, thirty-three years after independence, still haven't been able to choose their destiny freely. This, I'm sure you'll agree, constitutes a very serious obstacle. But, if it's all right with you, let's not get into that subject right now. Let's go back to your early political activities. Why did you stay for a year with the communists who infiltrated the Union nationale de la jeunesse algérienne [National Union of Algerian Youth], an F.L.N. organization?

K.M.: I found that I naturally sympathized with the communists, for reasons we've already discussed. It suited me quite well. To be honest, I adopted solidarity with the untouchable ex-U.S.S.R. without thinking. I was immersed in dogma, in an almost religious kind of behavior. But there was also a major current of democratic leftist thought on campus to which I was quite sensitive. The proponents of that movement were vitriolic in their criticism of the Algerian government. They denounced everything: corruption, the government's economic choices, industrialization, land reform, institutional and police totalitarianism, and the cultural and ideological references the state used to legitimize its decisions— like its narrow interpretation of Islam and its distorted version of Algeria's history.

But, you know, I'm an incorrigible pragmatist who has always been brought back down to earth by realities. And the realities, for me, were women and the Berber question. In our country, the well-known thesis on women that the entire left espoused during the 1970s depicted women's fight as neither specific nor a priority. Given that Algeria's basic problem was development, the liberation of women was seen as secondary to that of the workers, a group in which women were only one of many components. The woman who claimed the contrary and wanted to seize on this secondary question in order to make it a major issue was called a "moody *petite-bourgeoise.*" I came very quickly to disagree completely with that attitude, but I realized that one could not expect a patriarchal society to undergo a revolution in this area.

On another front, the Berber Spring broke out, in 1980. It was a pacifist movement aimed at reclaiming the Berbers' cultural and linguistic identity, which had been cruelly suppressed. My heart skipped a beat, as you can imagine! In a one-party system—which Kundera has described so well for the countries of Eastern Europe—a protest of this sort is a sign of democratic vitality. Now, the communists denounced the Berber cultural movement, claiming that it was engineered by Morocco's Hassan II and U.S. imperialists; I found that unacceptable! Rather, wasn't it the F.L.N. that was fooling around with the imperialists in question, since it had just signed a twenty-five year agreement with the American gasoline company El Paso? I had heated discussions on campus with Slimane M., the head of the clandestine group to which I belonged. The totalitarian spirit of communism, and its inability to answer the problems of a society like ours, hit me in the face. I was already uneasy: the "judicious support" that the Communist Party was lending to the government was, in fact, an unquestionable support. After a year, I broke definitively with the communists. I committed myself wholeheartedly to the feminist battle, alerted by the threats that were emerging.

E.S.: Do you mean that, as soon as Chadli took power, women became a target? Why was that?

K.M.: Chadli, in contrast to Boumediene*, was not a strong man who had seized power himself. He was the pawn of a clan, of a certain current in the F.L.N. and the army: namely, the Islamo-baasist* camp, which up to then had been in the minority but which ended up winning out over the socialist-modernists. The objective of this clan, beyond ensuring that Algerian assets continued to yield a profit to their benefit, was to place the country under the law of *charia*. To succeed, they had to launch a simultaneous attack on the three pillars on which they planned to base that project: women, education, and the justice system. In a few years, the "reform" would be carried out!

E.S.: But were you immediately aware of those intentions?

K.M.: No. It would take us some time to understand the true nature of the new team and its deep, hidden links to the Islamist International.

E.S.: How did the initial threats against women manifest themselves?

K.M.: At the very beginning of 1980, a ministerial order landed on our heads. It prohibited women from leaving the country unless they were accompanied by a male chaperon—even their son would do! Obviously, in a dictatorship, no one warns you about this sort of arbitrary decision. But it happened that some women teachers, who were enrolled in France for their theses and were getting ready to go see their advisors, were stopped at the airport and prevented from leaving. One of them invoked the Constitution that had been adopted by referendum in 1976 to argue that equality of the sexes and freedom of movement were guaranteed by law. She triggered a public scandal that was timidly echoed in the Francophone daily *El Moudjahid* and in the weekly *Algérie-Actualités*. Those of us at the university took our courage in both hands:

we decided to draw up an enormous petition and request a meeting with the Minister of the Interior. He met with us, which, in my eyes, already constituted a first victory. Our determination was absolute. So, on March 8, 1980, for International Women's Day, we organized a huge general assembly and decided to demonstrate in the streets, demanding that the order which hampered women's freedom of movement be definitively lifted. The government retreated: the ministerial order was canceled.

During this time, however, an item in a newspaper reported that the government was preparing a pilot study of the *Code sur le statut personnel* [Family Code*] that it hoped to present to the Assembly. It represented a very clear step back for women and would be totally unconstitutional. We went, a hundred strong, to stage a sit-in the offices of the U.N.F.A.* [National Union of Algerian Women, an organization run by the F.L.N.]. We wanted to get the classified text of this pilot study. The women of the Union replied: "Algerian women are not aware of their rights. Thus there's nothing to discuss"! So we formed a collective, the first one.

E.S.: How many of you were involved in this movement?

K.M.: About fifty.

E.S.: And then what happened?

K.M.: Throughout 1981, in spite of the repression, we continued. Some women at the ministry of the Plan informed us that the Code was ready to be debated in secret. On October 28, 1981, a hundred of us demonstrated in the streets. *El Moudjahid* carried the headline: "A Hundred Angry Women." On November 16, there were five hundred of us gathered in front of the Assembly as it met for a plenary session, and we had gathered more than ten thousand signatures of support from all over Algeria. Along with two friends, I marched into the Assembly chambers. Rabah Bitat, the Assembly president, whose wife—a war veteran and a lawyer—was with us, was obliged to adjourn the session. The assembly leaders skillfully manipulated the situation: we were given four days to "make propositions for amending the text," which was still confidential. The movement became divided at that point: there were those who wanted to accept the deal, and those who rejected it. On December 23, those of us in the latter camp gathered in Algiers, in front of the main post office. It was an important day.

E.S.: Why?

K.M.: Because the old *moudjahidat** who had led the fight for liberation within the F.L.N. joined us, the young, as a bloc, for the first time. Thirty of them decided to join the fight against a government that had completely betrayed them. Among them was the legendary Djamila Bouhired*. They formed a security cordon around us. We had some very good slogans on our signs—"No to the Family Code!" "No to Silence, Yes to Democracy!" and "No to the Betrayal of the Ideals of November 1, 1954!"—which the moudjahidat took up and used as the title of the open letter they wrote to Chadli a few days later. In the sympathetic crowd that was observing our demonstration, there were several old people who could be heard saying: "It's a good thing there are women in this country. They dare to do what men won't do." As for my mother, whom I had invited to come, she answered: "My dear, if I come, can you guarantee that your father will let me back in the house?"

E.S.: What impact did the moudjahidat's open letter have for the feminist movement?

K.M.: A big one, because it was the first time that Algerian women didn't merely say no to the government but also stated their rights themselves. They summarized those rights in six points: women should reach the age of legal majority at the same time as men, they should have an unconditional right to work, they should enjoy equality in marriage and in divorce, polygamy should be abolished, common inheritances should be equally divided, and abandoned children should be properly protected—that is, single mothers should have legal status.[1]

E.S.: Did Chadli give in?

K.M.: Yes, because the revolt of the "history-makers" put him in a difficult situation. He could not claim that this was a revolt led by women on the extreme left who sought to take revenge on the bourgeois government, or by feminists who were fighting a misogynous state. The moudjahidat are the most legitimate women in the eyes of the people. So Chadli withdrew the bill for the Code. For us, it was a great victory—but, unfortunately, a temporary one.

E.S.: In front of the main post office, two generations of women, mothers and daughters (symbolically at least) finally joined to-

---

1. The reader should note that adoption is illegal in Algeria. This summary illustrates that the Algerian feminist movement is, first and foremost, a civil rights movement.

gether in 1981. Why had the moudjahidat stayed out of sight for almost twenty years?

K.M.: I asked them the same question myself. They answered that they had never stopped being militants, but that their work was not public. They had been working primarily on behalf of the mistreated orphans and widows of the war. But they added: "The war of liberation was very hard, murderous, and painful. We had no family life ..." What that means is that they were ready to go back "inside." When men asked them to do so, they complied—out of weariness, and because they had a right to rest and have children. At one moment in our conversations, they also admitted: "We never, never would have imagined that the men next to whom we'd fought would lead our country in such a way, or do to us what they are doing." One of them, who is, unfortunately, unwilling to write down her experiences in a book, told me: "Our return to 'the inside' didn't begin in 1962, but, rather, before independence. Little by little, during the war, the F.L.N. removed us from the real fighting zones and sent us to the borders or overseas. Our role was defined from that moment on. We didn't have any place in the world of the 'outside.'"

E.S.: What happened to Djamila Bouhired, the woman who planted bombs for the F.L.N. during the Algerian war, who was tortured and condemned to death by colonial France, and who was also the wife of Jacques Vergès*?

K.M.: Would you believe it, I ran into her again by chance in 1991. I was in a store in Algiers, and I was facing away from the door when I heard this voice that I would have recognized anywhere. I turned around and saw a big woman wearing sunglasses. "Are you Djamila Bouhired?" "What? ... You recognize me?" She took off her glasses. "Ah! ... But you're Khalida Messaoudi!" She started to cry, and I myself was deeply moved. The F.I.S. was already forcing women to wear the veil, and persecuting, burning, whipping them. I will never forget it. She took me in her arms and said: "My daughter, what troubled times they're putting you through! Be brave, don't give up!"

E.S.: What happened between the moment when Chadli retreated in the face of the moudjahidat and June 9, 1984, the date when the Family Code began to be applied after being adopted by the Assembly in the month of May?

K.M.: What happened was that we weren't as good as our elders. We thought that the government had definitively retreated and wouldn't dare impose on us this wicked and shamefully backward Code in the name of a gang of scoundrels who were running Algeria as if it were their plaything. We were all secularists who believed in the separation of church and state and who were fighting for citizenship. We wanted to use that fight to gain a bit more equality and justice for women. We returned to the idea of writing a manifesto on the rights of women, a project that some in our group had proposed back in 1980, and we decided to take the time necessary to gather as many signatures as possible. It is very difficult, you know, to work only by word of mouth, especially in such a big country. The F.L.N. didn't allow us access to any mode of communication. Never. We were reduced to improvising, which was risky for all of us. And we had to be patient about gathering the million signatures we were counting on. That was a fatal mistake on our part, because the government, which had eyes and ears everywhere, began to strike. The repression swooped down on us in December 1983: the police charged into all the covert parties and arrested everyone, four militant women in particular. For four months, we mobilized all our energies to spread the word about these imprisonments as best we could. Then the Code was adopted, in haste, without our being able to do anything about it. A few months later, everyone was freed, as if by chance!

E.S.: What, exactly, is contained in this Code?

K.M.: In this Code, Algerian women exist henceforth only as "daughters of," "mothers of," or "wives of." They are not individuals in their own right. On five points—education, work, marriage, divorce, and inheritance—this text makes them eternal minors, who go from dependency on their father, brother, or closest male relative to dependency on their husband.

The text of the Code says nothing about the right to education and to work. The only role it assigns to woman is that of procreator who reproduces her husband's name and protects his well-being along with that of his relatives. Women are thereby trapped in a situation in which they must constantly negotiate their other rights. For example, a man who wants his wife to stop working can force her to stop, because she owes him obedience (article 39).

As for marriage, whether a woman is single, divorced, a widow with or without children, illiterate, educated, a housewife, a magistrate, or a minister, she can never arrange a marriage herself (article 11). Women are dispossessed of this right, which is handed over to a matrimonial guardian who can abuse his power. To get a full sense of how profoundly revolting all this is, let's take the case of Leïla Aslaoui, an exceptional woman who is a symbol on the Algerian political scene. Here is an important magistrate—a woman who had vitriol thrown on her by the fundamentalists during the 1980s, who was named minister in 1991-92 and again in 1994, and whose husband, a dentist, had his throat savagely cut in his office by the armed wing of the F.I.S. in November 1994—who, if she wanted to remarry one day, would be obliged to go through the law of the matrimonial guardian. Do you realize what sort of choice is left to women in Algeria, between the infamous Code and fundamentalist barbarism? And that's not the end of it! Not only are women not free to arrange their own marriages, but they must live under a sword of Damocles: polygamy, a shameful privilege that men are guaranteed by article 8. Polygamy has nothing to do with a married man having mistresses, an argument I've often heard used by both Western men and Islamists. The only things common to the two situations are masculine desire and its appeasement. But the multiple wives and concubines that exist don't choose their status: they are enslaved in legal terms, often bound hand and foot in economic terms, and never free in sexual terms. Sadly, do the women who are subjected to polygamy ever get to speak out? How could they, given that they are condemned to silence? ...

Divorce, of course, can occur through mutual consent, or at a woman's request, but only in cases that are, in practice, impossible to prove (article 53). By contrast, a man needs only to desire a divorce in order to get one. Without any conditions. As I'm sure you can see, we're talking about an abusive, unilateral divorce—a repudiation that dares not speak its name. I almost forgot to tell you about the practice of *khol'â*, which allows a woman to divorce on the condition that she give up any claim to alimony. Khol'â is the problematic ransom that women must pay for their freedom, just like slaves. As for the effects of divorce, they are dramatic for both women and children. The mother automatically has the right to custody, but not the right to be her children's guardian: the father's signature is necessary for everything, absolutely everything, from enrollment in school or at the local swimming pool to authorization to leave the country. She can never find housing, in reality. First of all, when there is only one residence for the two spouses, it always goes to the husband, without the possibility of any recourse (article 52, line 3). Then, supposing that the family owns several residences, the husband typically skirts the law by temporarily signing the other residences over to a third party, just for the duration of the divorce. The dirty trick is pulled off! On top of that, in the current climate of unprecedented economic crisis and soaring poverty, fewer and fewer families are able to take in these divorced women and their children. A dramatic phenomenon has thus arisen in the ten years since the Code has been in force: thousands of mothers wander through the streets with their kids, and the state couldn't care less about them. An association called "S.O.S. Women in Distress," which is literally collapsing under the weight of the cries for help it receives, can only manage to respond to a fraction of those requests, for lack of means.

Finally, on the subject of inheritance, the legislators imposed full charia upon us: the man has the right to twice as much as the woman. And this is done on the pretext that we are in a Muslim society. But if the argument of the state were fair, then why have the majority of Muslim countries abolished slavery (to my great satisfaction ...)—a practice that is perfectly legal from the point of view of charia? And why did the authorities convene *ouléma** to produce *fatwas** that make bank interest legal, when it is forbidden by Islam? In fact, charia is brandished just as readily by the government as by the Algerian fundamentalists when it suits their purposes. In this case, it is used to justify the oppression of women. All these men—supported by the women who back them—are scared out of their wits by equality: they are afraid that it would make them lose their supremacy, not their souls, as they claim.

E.S.: How did the "debates" on the Code unfold in the one-party Assembly?

K.M.: They began, as I told you, in 1981. They were not public. But what was already happening in *El Moudjahid* was scandalous. This newspaper reported, for example, that a deputy had proposed that the Code determine by law the length of the stick with which a man could beat his wife. I have in my possession a copy of the *Official Journal* of the debates that took place in 1984, right before the text was adopted. The first thing we should note is that the overwhelming majority of the references made by our "deputies" are not to the Constitution but to charia and the most reactionary interpretation of the Koran and of the Sunna, the Tradition of the Prophet! Thus one of the Code's zealous sponsors, Abdelaziz Belkhadem—a member of the F.L.N.'s Political Bureau to this very day, former president of the Assemblée-croupion* [Rump Assembly], artisan of the deal between the F.L.N. and the F.I.S. that took place under Chadli's reign in 1991, and one of the most important promoters of the "dialogue" with the fundamentalists today—went so far as to propose that women be assigned to a forced residence. He did so in the name of the *sura** entitled "The Confederates," or, rather, of his interpretation of it. Furthermore, Belkhadem categorically rejected the idea of a modern Islam that could coexist with the ideals of liberty, equality, and citizenship. He concluded by saying: "The sincere Muslim is one who conforms to charia in its entirety. [. . .] There is no ancient, or medieval, or modern, or progressive Islam, there is only one Islam." What he meant by that was his Islam, the Islam of Abassi Madani*, of Ali Benhadj*, of the Pakistani El Mawdoudi, of the Sudanese Tourabi, and company ... These sentences, among others, would crop up again in the pronouncements and written propaganda of Islamists all over the world. In 1984, when I was looking for fundamentalists in the street, I was looking in the wrong place: they were in the legislative branch of the government. I realized this afterward. The Family Code is to the fundamentalists and the F.I.S. what a marriage contract is to couples.

E.S.: It must be hard to forgive yourself for failing to keep such a bill from becoming law ...

K.M.: I had the feeling that the deepest injustice had been perpetrated. We had been had, totally had, and we could do nothing but bang our heads against the wall, because we knew that this text was going to structure the entire society from that point on. For me, the whole business had really opened my eyes: the traitor in this story was the Algerian state. For, at the moment when our confrontation over the Code took place, there had only been the government and our group of three hundred women, plus a few magistrates and lawyers. Only a handful of interested parties were there. Algerians couldn't have given a damn. There hadn't even been any Islamists outside, saying "We want charia to be applied," because their representatives were in the Assembly. Yes, the traitor who wanted the Code and imposed it on everyone was clearly the state. Toward women, it was fundamentalist. And its schizophrenia—having one foot in modernity, through its programs for the economy and industrialization, and one foot in obscurantism, through its behavior toward us—was bound to produce mutants. What I mean by "mutants" are the young people who are unemployed and utterly lacking in roots and values, who are torn between a tradition that has been reduced to a few traces and upheavals that go in all directions without bringing stability to anyone. It's enough to drive you crazy, and that's what happened. These young people threw themselves into the arms of the F.I.S., when they should have been checking themselves into psychiatric hospitals.

E.S.: During the three years when your movement was fighting the Family Code, how did men behave?

K.M.: You make me laugh! Aside from a few rare exceptions, there were no men in our movement! ... Men were painfully absent from our struggle. This reinforced my conviction that Algerian women could expect salvation only from themselves. Some men tried to take over our struggle, by using women who belonged to the parties of the left and extreme left; for them, we were interesting as a base of operation that might help them attain their own objectives. Other men called us "imperialist lackeys." Finally, there were men who saw us as killjoys, as people who were holding back the process of "setting priorities." In Algeria, as in all totalitarian regimes, it's always like that: whatever you do, you're always slandered. That attitude is typical of the infantile political behavior fostered by a dictatorship. Rumor takes the place of information. We're paying dearly for the fact that we don't have any tradition of civic struggle.

E.S.: Do you mean to say that the lack of organization evident among Algerian men can also be explained by their own status?

K.M.: Certainly. Our men's patriarchal, lordly, and misogynous behavior doesn't provide all the keys to explaining it. Algerian men went directly from subjugation under colonial France, to a war of liberation in which all debate was prohibited, and then to thirty years of single-party politics. They, too, were excluded from political life by the F.L.N. and the army, excluded from speaking freely. They accepted it and didn't rise up in protest, except for a few young men like Saïd Sadi*. So when a woman, when women come along and say: "I want, we want to have a role in this political life," they force men to recognize their own impotence. They reflect back the image of the men's guilty silence. They castrate them, without wanting to, of course. Suddenly, the majority of men are overcome with hatred toward women. Very few of them admit that women are opening up healthy spaces of liberty, or that their demonstrations are wonderful precedents.

E.S.: Do you think their attitude is similar to that of the historians who focus on Algeria, particularly French historians? I ask that because not a single historian, to my knowledge, has given Algerian women their due. It is as if, from the war of liberation to the battle for democracy, women didn't exist!

K.M.: Listen, Elisabeth ... For me, the situation is clear. Apart from the Berber cultural movement, it has been women—yes, women, and they alone—who have been publicly questioning the F.L.N. since 1980–81 and demanding that universal principles be enforced. Do you realize what holding four demonstrations in quick succession to demand freedom, equality, and citizenship represents in a country where no one talks about the Algerian personality except as something forged by Islam and Arabism? Well, those historians you mention, whether they are Algerians in exile or French, have the same reactions ingrained in their minds as do all other men. As soon as they see a woman in Algeria, they go blind. For them, you remain under your veil, in the harem of their phantasms—which never existed in our country. This is particularly true of leftist historians ... In certain books that are accepted as authoritative, when the demonstrations that have mattered in Algeria are discussed, it is symptomatic that not a single allusion is made to women's demonstrations. Moreover, a new phenomenon has appeared recently: any woman whose political pronouncements don't correspond to their scheme of things is immediately doomed to symbolic lynching and stoning. Scholars, who are all the more dangerous for having an academic and intellectual authority, suddenly transform themselves into ideologues, into preachers of hate, and employ insult, anathema, and defamation. It's pitiful, but not discouraging.

E.S.: During the years when you were fighting the Code, you met your future husband, a teacher. Now, you declared earlier that you didn't see yourself in the role of wife, and that you would probably prefer a free union. So why did you end up following tradition?

K.M.: I followed it without following it. That is, I got married, of course, but to a man who was not a *marabout** and who didn't belong in any way to my clan. I broke with the tradition of endogamy. It was time to open the window and let in some fresh air! Moreover, we had a civil wedding ceremony, at the town hall. However, to make my father happy, I consented to have a religious ceremony as well. I should, however, point out that, in my circle, that doesn't mean a marriage in a mosque as is common today. Rather, it is a private, family affair, where the maternal uncle officiates. This was at the end of the 1970s. It was a time when it was possible to satisfy everyone, secularists and practicing Muslims alike, without a problem. The state hadn't yet starting interfering in people's private lives, and hadn't yet mixed up politics and religion, as it was soon to do with the Code.

E.S.: You still haven't explained why you got married ...

K.M.: In my mind, it was settled. While taking care to protect the convictions and sensibilities of my parents, I had moved quite far away from the notion that "you must stay pure and virginal." I was very lucky because my future husband, being a teacher, already had a room and was soon to have an apartment. Do you realize what a privilege that is in an overpopulated country where available housing is painfully short? I have to say that, in Algeria, it is almost impossible for a girl and boy, or a man and woman, to find a decent place to make love. There's no place where you can be intimate with someone. There is always someone watching you. Always ...

E.S.: What about hotels?

K.M.: You must be joking! A couple can't check in to a hotel room unless they're married, unless they present an official family record book. Even if they take the precaution of asking for two separate rooms to allay suspicion, if the hotel clerk thinks anything is abnormal, he calls the police right away. As for a single woman who reserves a hotel room, she is immediately pointed out to the cops. We were able to escape from that. But we lived in an apartment complex. And the complex was spying on us, just as it spies on everyone. My companion couldn't stand it any more, and he was very afraid for me—afraid that the neighbors would denounce me. So I married him, so that the neighborhood would leave us in peace.

E.S.: In sum, you gave in to cultural pressure, exactly like the girls who wear the veil ...

K.M.: First of all, not all the girls who wear the veil do it under pressure ... As for me, I did, in fact, give in to the stifling environment. A moment came when, in the society in which I found myself—a society that was the singular product of a particular history—I had to make a choice. For me to confront that society head-on as a free thinker, I would have had to have the temperament and status of someone like Kateb Yacine*, which is not the case. The alternative was to try to transform society through a slow and collective approach that didn't exclude individual compromises. It seems to me that I didn't lose anything—neither my convictions nor my soul—by taking the second route.

E.S.: Did your husband, a liberal militant, support you in your feminist struggle?

K.M.: Yes. He supported me intellectually. But the problem, for each of us, was always following through on a commitment, when life made us confront our principles. Have you seen very many privileged people say spontaneously: "I renounce my privileges"? So, when we decided to get a divorce a few years later in 1991, the Family Code had been adopted and had the force of law. I no longer had any legal right to our conjugal residence, since it was handed over to my husband. We made a deal. My fate was less odious than that of the vast majority of women, but I was humiliated to have to negotiate my dignity, my status as a human being in my own right. I resented the state far more than I resented my husband. That's all I'll say about that. It's a private matter.

E.S.: After the Family Code was adopted, what did the feminist movement do?

K.M.: From the moment when the Code had the force of law, we could no longer settle for having our battle orchestrated by an informal committee. The movement had to have a permanent, efficient framework. This new structure had to be legal and recognized. We fought for that, with a single thing in mind: abolishing the Code. On May 16, 1985, forty of us—women of all political sensibilities and from all the regions of the country—gathered in Algiers for a luncheon. And we founded the Association for Legal

Equality Between Women and Men, which would last until 1989, having been neither authorized nor forbidden. Contrary to what I read in the January 1995 issue of the journal *Esprit*, in an article written by Mohamed Harbi and Monique Gadan, it was by no means Trotskyists who were responsible for creating this association, and one of the women they named as its founders [Louisa Hannoun*] didn't join us until later. Most of us were women who were not tied to political parties—that is, to the men who set the strategies for those parties. Once again, well-meaning people have falsified history.

E.S.: In that same issue of *Esprit*, this is said about you: "My first impulse is to admire the courage of this woman, who risks her life by speaking with her face uncovered, knowing that a large part of Algeria, and not only her friends, are watching this television program through their satellite dishes. Then I think about all those women in Algeria, in the countryside or in the city suburbs: what can this television appearance mean for them? I imagine that, even if they approve of her courage and her ideas, her persona can't affect them deeply. She is a woman who has succeeded, who apparently isn't married, who has no husband and no children, and she's a woman who asserts her power in front of men: women viewers must find it difficult to identify with her, or to believe that an Algerian woman should be like that ..."

K.M.: First of all, has anyone ever asked someone like Abdelhamid Mehri, the secretary general of the F.L.N., if he is married and how many children he has? Just to reassure those who are traumatized by sterility, Mehri is not only a husband but a father as well. That doesn't in the least change this man's unpopularity, or the hatred Algerians feel toward the party he represents, which is synonymous with corruption, the misuse of public funds, assassinations, chaos, mediocrity—in a word, with disaster. In keeping with tradition, Mehri's personal status doesn't make him any more legitimate.

As for the gist of that commentary, I've never done an opinion poll of Algerian women and thus don't know whether they see me as their representative, and I've never run for elected office,[2] which would have given me a chance to determine my popularity or unpopularity. Let's remember, too, that no one knows what Al-

2. See "Recent Elections in Algeria" in the Glossary.

gerian women would say if they were truly allowed to express themselves freely, without their father, or husband, or brother, or imam looking over their shoulder. I'm ready to bet that, in those conditions, they would say that they are in favor of education, the right to work, and liberty. So I can answer only on the basis of some personal observations.

Number 1. Algerian women are going through one of the most catastrophic economic situations, in that fewer than 4 percent of them are employed.

Number 2. 56 percent are illiterate.

Number 3. They all live under the law known as the Family Code, which means that they no longer have the protection of the traditional system, nor that of the state.

Number 4. They are subjected to fundamentalist barbarism.

Given the state of exclusion in which Algerian women live, and the constant supervision and terrorism to which they are subject, what do I propose to them? That they stand up to the government by insisting that the Code be repealed and demanding that egalitarian civil rights be promulgated; that they fight the dominant patriarchal values; and that they fight the Islamists. Obviously, not all women have the means or the psychological and familial support necessary to lead this three-way battle. But would it be fair or acceptable for the women who do have those means, like me, to shrink from the fight? Why should we assume that a given model for Algerian women is invalid simply because it isn't the most widespread? Why should these women be condemned to identifying exclusively with models of submission? In the name of what should those women—Algerian women, and more generally Muslim women—who have the insolence to say "I" publicly, the courage to express themselves and reject the veil, and to speak out in defense of the values of liberty, equality, and secularism, be condemned straightaway to internal exile, to being stripped of their identity?

Now, there are other questions to address. Should one, following the example of Stalin, ask, "Khalida Messaoudi, how many divisions have you assembled?" in order for me to be credible? Some people raise the objection that I am in the minority. So be it. Since when, in the history of societies, has the justness of a point of view or a cause been measured by the number of its supporters? Were the twenty-two men who decided to launch the war of liberation in Algeria, in 1954, wrong because there were only twenty-two of them? In Revolutionary France, Olympe de Gouges was decapitated because she defended the rights of women and blacks. Was she wrong for doing that? And did the fact that Hitler was brought to power by millions of votes in a national election make him right?

E.S.: But aren't you underestimating the extent to which women have internalized the obligations Islam imposes on them?

K.M.: First of all, the traditional patriarchal system in Algeria is more powerful than Islam, and it has proven that. Indeed, Islam was forced to superpose itself onto preexisting socioeconomic structures. Second, outside its five pillars—the profession of faith, prayer, Ramadan, *zakat** [alms-giving], and the pilgrimage to Mecca for those who can manage it—Islam has as many obligations as schools of interpretation. Thus, in Algeria, the Mozabite woman, who is just as Muslim as the Chaoui* woman, is confined to the home, whereas the Chaoui woman can go out because she is obliged to feed her family. To give another example, entire regions have deprived their women of education, whereas among the Touareg, who are just as Muslim as anyone else, it is women who are literate and who are entrusted with the task of transmitting culture and writing because they are sedentary. So you see that the values that are internalized are those of the forces that dominate in a given society, even if those values are justified and legitimized by religious leaders. When Bourguiba of Tunisia decided to promote the equality of the sexes in 1956, he summoned ouléma and asked them to figure out a way to make that equality legitimate through an interpretation of the sacred text. And that is what happened. Tunisian women have never thought that they lost their culture, their patrimony, or their faith because of this.

E.S: And what about the power that you supposedly assert in front of men?

K.M.: That sort of question really doesn't concern me. And if women were in power, the Family Code would be long gone! Would the author of that remark, whom I don't know, call "power" the fact that I speak up and don't always say "Anaâm, sidi"—"Very good, your Majesty"?

Chapter 6
Khomeini? Never Heard of Him!

Elisabeth Schemla: During the years we've been discussing, a major event occurred in the Muslim world: the Iranian revolution. Its consequences were terrible for an entire people, and particularly for its women. I suppose that, to strengthen your thinking and your battle, you closely observed Khomeini's rise to power?

Khalida Messaoudi: I'd like to be able to answer "yes" to your question. Unfortunately, that is not at all the case.

E.S.: Do you mean to suggest that you took no note of this event?

K.M.: Absolutely. The same is true of almost all the Algerian women who were involved in the feminist struggle, and they weren't alone. I'll try, honestly, to clear up this paradox. First of all, we were living under a regime in which the state controlled the information we received. On the radio, on the television, and in the newspapers, we were bombarded with the official line: "Long live the Iranian revolution!," "Long live Khomeini!" The media exalted the triumph of a nationalist and Muslim liberation movement over American imperialism. Moreover, the government systematically censored all mention of the attacks on human rights that Khomeini committed: the thousands of public hangings, the arrests, torture, and so on. That was our only source of information. You can't find French newspapers in Algeria, and in any case my generation is not very attuned to the French press because we grew up without it. Besides, was the French press truly reporting on the real situation in Iran? Didn't French journalists, as a group, also try to hide their faces before the mullahs, just as they're doing today before the F.I.S.*? And let's not forget that Algeria was acting at that time as an intermediary to release the funds needed for the revolution, and played a crucial role between Iraq and Iran during the conflict, offering its good offices when the hostages were taken at the American Embassy. Power politics were not foreign to the government's attitude ... Finally, because of our own history, our war of liberation, Algerians are automatically sympathetic toward any revolution, whether it be Cuban, Vietnamese, or Iranian.

E.S.: Do you really believe that the gag rule that was applied to news coverage suffices to explain your blindness as to what was going on in Iran?

K.M.: Remember that we're talking about a leftist movement ... In the "Women" collective I told you about, we had some debates at the very beginning of the Iranian revolution. The vast majority of women teachers supported the "victory of the popular masses over the national and international bourgeoisie." As I recall, there were only three in our group who were up in arms; they declared that a revolution that buries women by forcing them to wear the veil cannot by any means be considered liberating. They even predicted that the consequences would be dreadful, especially for women who had symbolic status, like artists and intellectuals ... One of them flung this retort at us: "Let's make an appointment for ten years from now, and we'll see what will have come of your revolution!" These poor women wrote a tract in support of Iranian women and then went out all by themselves to put a copy in every mailbox in Algiers! I didn't budge, even though I vaguely sensed that they were right. I stuck to the sledgehammer argument that we used against them: "Iranians are Shiites, whereas we are Sunni Muslims,[1] so we'll never fall into that trap." Deep down, I admitted that, as far as women were concerned, I didn't see very much difference between Sunnis and Shiites. Nonetheless, I didn't want to think about all that: Iran was far, very far away from us, both geographically and intellectually. I stuck with that position, and then we stopped talking about it altogether. In a word, I buried my head in the sand.

E.S.: Do you feel guilty?

K.M.: I feel worse than that. I allowed myself to be taken in by a

---

1. See "Islam in Algeria" in the Glossary.

criminal blindness. Today, when I am pained by all the rapes and assassinations committed against women and girls by the F.I.S., I find my reaction indecent. Because I refused to see what was happening in Iran, I didn't give myself the means of averting the death of these Algerian women, of preventing Katia Bengana from losing her life at the age of seventeen because she didn't want to wear a veil ...

Today, when I see certain writers assert, for example, that in Algeria a class conflict is pitting a bourgeois government against a populist Islamist opposition, I feel like hitting someone. But then I tell myself: "Didn't you do the same thing about the Iranians? Didn't you subscribe to a Marxist reading of that event, which suited you just as it suited everyone else? Didn't you prefer the comfort of your intellectual interpretation?" I see my own cowardice in a certain number of people from the West and from the Maghreb whose support I now seek but fail to get. I recognize it. I recognize what was my own propensity to apply categories, concepts, and analytical grids that exempt one from feeling any solidarity. But my own defection on the subject of Iranian women taught me not to judge this lack of solidarity toward my struggle. I am still as ashamed as ever for having abandoned the women of Iran, and I'd like to rush to their aid. But the only way I can support them now is by speaking out and underscoring that the veil of our silence adds to the veil of terror the mullahs have imposed on them. Thousands and thousands of women were jailed by the commandos of the *pasdahan**, for having a *hidjab** with a lock of hair peeking out or in the wrong color. Women are stoned under a law that specifies everything right down to the size of the rock that should be used for the stoning.[2] Here, look at the document yourself. The tragedy is that I can no longer do anything for these women, because in Algeria I'm now in the same situation as they are ... Fundamentally, we are facing the same system of totalitarianism based on religious arguments. There the system has been in place for fifteen years, and the "masses" are more crushed than

---

2. The testimony Messaoudi gave at the International Women's Conference (Vienna, 1993), concerning the persecution of women in Iran and Sudan as well as in Algeria, is reprinted in "La Nouvelle Inquisition," *Les Temps Modernes* (January–February 1995): 213–22.

ever. Here, the system is threatening to take hold because we have collectively closed our eyes.

E.S.: While you were closing your eyes, weren't the fundamentalists immediately drawing the lessons that could be drawn from Khomeini's rise to power?

K.M.: Obviously! But it took me two years just to begin to realize that. I needed to have a certain distance to understand that the Khomeini revolution had opened the door to all sorts of possibilities for the Algerian Islamist movement. The revolution proved to those involved in that movement that the conquest of power not only was possible but could be done rapidly, simply by seizing the necessary means. And that is exactly what the fundamentalists set out to do, without me or anyone else being able to piece together the apparently unconnected signs of their new strategy. The Islamists reorganized themselves, covertly. They intensified the *Daâwa** [proselytism] and their indoctrination of crowds, so that the masses would be ready to impose the Islamic state on the chosen day. They also decided to harass the regime, on two fronts. On the political front, the fundamentalists favored the emergence of charismatic figures who embodied the nation, like Abassi Madani*. And on the military front, they created an armed organization whose objective was to seize the reins, through violence if necessary. But how could I, on my campus, discern all that?

E.S.: You weren't able to analyze the rise of fundamentalism. That may be easy to say in hindsight, but even so ... As early as 1975, there had been violent confrontations at the Law School in Algiers between progressive and Islamist students. In 1982 a student named Kamal Amzal was hacked and stabbed to death by a fundamentalist group in the Ben-Aknoun student residence, and twelve other young people were injured. Attacks were taking place in university student centers and dormitories all over the country. During this period a secret organization, the Algerian Islamic Movement [M.I.A.*] was created by Mustafa Bouyali. These fundamentalists broke into quarries to steal dynamite and seized some weapons here and there. Then they took to the bush: the incident made quite a stir. In 1984 an impressive demonstration was triggered in Kouba by the funeral of Soltani, one of the ideologues of Algerian Islamism. Finally, in 1985, the followers of Bouyali attacked the largest Algerian police academy in Soumaâ, between

Algiers and Blida. Even in a dictatorial regime where the press was muzzled, people knew about all this. So, how much attention did you pay to these events, while you yourself were fighting the Family Code*?

K.M.: I was revolted, outraged by the assassination of Kamal Amzal. And I was quite preoccupied by all this growing fundamentalist violence. But I certainly wasn't aware of the real danger. It's rather complicated to explain. Yet I think it's important to find a way to explain our mindset in 1984-85, because it resembles the way we were thinking in 1990, when we stupidly believed that the F.I.S. had no chance of winning the municipal elections, or the legislative elections in 1991.

First of all, our group, which was composed of students and teachers from the left or extreme left and some Berberist militants, was alone on the playing field. On the university campuses, our tracts and posters were plastered on all the walls, and we were in charge of all the committees. We were completely absorbed in the hatred we felt toward the F.I.S. and, in our eyes, the only fight that was worthy of Algeria was the fight for democracy. We were convinced that this model was the only one that could bring down the single-party government, and that it was the best remedy against totalitarianism. We had no doubt that democracy would be the next step in the history of our country. At the same time, the cops were spying on us, hounding us, and hunting us down for the slightest little photocopy, for the slightest pamphlet calling for a "League on Human Rights," which we tried to distribute. In May 1981, for example, they arrested all the leaders of the democratic movement at the University of Algiers. The repression was very severe, and we had to struggle to survive. So, when Kamal Amzal was assassinated by an Islamist militia that included several elements from outside the university, we were disoriented by the prospect of facing another type of violence. And even if the murderers of Kamal were arrested, what prevailed in our minds was—by far, by very far, Elisabeth—a terrible, devastating feeling of injustice. In fact, the government considered the fundamentalists far less dangerous than we democrats, and didn't give us a moment's rest! We could see this merely by observing our campus. After Amzal's assassins were arrested, three Islamist leaders, Madani, Sahnoun, and Soltani, called for a demonstration to protest their imprisonment. They called upon Chadli*, among others, to strengthen the Arabization of the school system, ban the sale of alcohol, and ... regulate individual rights in a manner that conformed more closely to *charia**! Do you see what I mean? I repeat that this was in 1982, two years before the Family Code was adopted. So what did Chadli do? He arrested them ... and freed them a few days later.

Here's another example. When the democratic students I was telling you about were arrested by the government, the Islamists took over all the committees. When our friends were released and asked for new elections at the university, the *Barbus* ["Bearded Ones"] refused: they denied that a democratic vote had any legitimacy and didn't mind proclaiming it. When some students tried to set up a roadblock to keep them out, they took bicycle chains to those who were blocking them and wounded several people. The government let them get away with it. Another time, they decided to annex one of the university's four study areas and turn it into a prayer room. Once again the students counterattacked, but in vain. An order was given to leave the room to the fundamentalists.

We also knew what was happening in the rest of Algeria. The government abandoned the management of the mosques to the Islamists. The Islamists shrewdly devised a way of circumventing the rule which required that every completed mosque be placed under the control of the Ministry of Religious Affairs, which represented institutional Islam. And the F.L.N.* didn't make any protest. There were thousands of such places of worship whose walls resounded with inflammatory sermons against women, culture, music, "Western morality," drinking, and, of course, the state itself—even though the government was, practically speaking, their ally. Do you know who was the imam of the mosque that was closest to my home, in the Baranès apartment complex, at this time? Mahfoudh Nahnah, the future president of the Algerian Hamas* ... In the mosques the fundamentalists handed out tracts and little political books that called for the creation of an Islamic state. In the basements of these mosques, young people were being trained in combat sports. During this period, from the late 1970s to the first half of the 1980s, the F.L.N. authorized only two types of associations: sporting associations ... and religious associations! We were dealing with a very tight network, with parallel circuits that the government tolerated even as it was crushing us. And it tolerated those circuits because it thought that it could control them and use them against us, the democratic, secular opponents who refused this exclusive Arabo-Muslim identity and the dictatorship its proponents wanted to impose on Algeria. It was also during this time that Chadli began his educational reform program, which effectively handed the schools over to the fundamentalists: we were better placed than anyone to realize that. So how could we help feeling heavy-hearted, first of all toward the corrupted officials who were in control? We understood, of course, that the Islamists were totalitarians—you didn't need to be a genius to figure that out! But, even though we were fully aware that they were working with the complicity of the state, we didn't imagine they could become a true political force ... We completely underestimated the fact that they were in the process of exploiting for their own benefit the economic failure of the F.L.N. and the impoverishment of the masses, and that the left had, little by little, lost touch with this general discontentment. Because we were persuaded that democracy was the way of the future, we believed, without thinking, that once the Algerian people got accustomed to freedom, they would recognize the madness of the fundamentalists. That was a major mistake!

E.S.: So are Algerians responsible, in your view, for the emergence of Islamic totalitarianism in their land?

K.M.: How could anyone claim the contrary? Although it is undeniably true that Saudi Arabia and Iran, the leaders of the two Islamist Internationals, supported and financed the Algerian fundamentalist movements, who allowed them to do so? We, the Algerians, did—either out of ideological complicity, pure and simple, or because we had set in place all the conditions that allowed them to interfere in our affairs, or because we underestimated the danger. We have to accept that first responsibility. Shying away from it would jeopardize our ability to think, to reflect upon the ties between Islam and politics, and between religion and the state. For more than thirty years we've been living in a kind of intellectual and psychological madness that has been organized and maintained by the regime, and that consists in completely shifting blame onto someone else. But wasn't it Chadli who, as of 1982, increased our contacts with Saudi Arabia and authorized that country's Islamic League to become more openly active in Algeria?

Ever since I grew up a bit, my first objection has always been to say: "It is we, and not someone else, who are despicable!" This may be somewhat excessive, but if you don't do that in Algeria, you lose your spirit. And it's not a question of self-flagellation. It's just a question of having the courage to love ourselves enough as Algerians to be able to look ourselves in the face, see what is wrong, and fix it. Whatever one may say about them, writers, novelists, playwrights, artists, intellectuals, and journalists have done this, and they are all the more admirable for it.

E.S.: When did you finally open your eyes about Iran?

K.M.: I didn't wake up until 1989, when Algerian women began to be persecuted by the Islamists. And when, during the same period, I finally met some Iranian women who had fled their country and settled in the West. They confirmed the reports of the network called "Women Living Under Muslim Law," which collected all the testimony it could obtain on what was happening in Iran, and also in Iraq, Pakistan, Afghanistan, and Bangladesh. 1989 ... For us, that was the beginning of the great upheaval.

Chapter 7
A Teacher During the Upheaval

Elisabeth Schemla: In 1982, with all your diplomas in hand, you became a math teacher. You started your teaching career in a rather curious way ...

Khalida Messaoudi: What you mean is, I didn't start it! I was assigned to a position forty kilometers from Algiers. Because I didn't have a car, and given the condition of Algeria's public transportation, it was impossible for me to accept this assignment. But, because I didn't trust the pen-pushers who made the rules, I inquired at several high schools in Algiers and found out that there were positions available. I ran like a shot to the Academy and explained my situation, but the guy who heard my story said: "I don't give a damn!" And he put me on unpaid leave for a year! There you have it, the Algeria of the F.L.N.*, where corruption was generalized and no one cared at all about the interests of the students. Bureaucrats blocked teaching positions and reserved them for the people they knew, who were supposed to return the favor by doing something for them or their family. Right away, to be able to eat, I began tutoring, since there are no private schools in Algeria. What my story shows, just to say it in passing, is that if the state does not respect teaching, you have no way out, whether you're a student or a teacher ...

E.S.: In 1983, you were assigned to a working-class high school in your neighborhood. You would stay there for three years. But your relations with the headmaster were stormy. Why?

K.M.: Here again, I was dealing with a corrupt system. This headmaster was a former *moudjahid** who became a teacher on the basis of that alone. Thanks to his F.L.N. card, he was promoted to the head of the establishment, without having any competence.

Ideologically, he was completely committed to defending the one-party system, and we got along very badly. In the end he got me, in 1986, because of a difference of opinion over our conception of patriotism.

E.S.: What happened?

K.M.: At the beginning of the 1984 school year, this man applied a ministerial decision: he ordered that the practice of raising and lowering the colors be followed in the high school on the first and last days of the week. Doesn't that remind you of the practices of all the "national this-or-thats," from Pétain to Saddam Hussein? So, on Thursday mornings, we had to have our students file out at ten to noon and, after calling the roll, make them stand there for a good fifteen minutes while they watched the flag being lowered and sang the national anthem. This was mandatory, even though they had the baccalauréat exam coming up and Thursday mornings were the time for doing review and synthesis exercises. I felt I had a responsibility to my students. One day, I was fed up with these stupidities, so I explained my position to my kids at great length and decided that we wouldn't leave our classroom before noon. In the courtyard, all the classes were lined up and waiting for us. The headmaster made a very vulgar gesture to me in front of everyone. I reacted strongly. He said to me: "Your refusal to attend the ceremony of the colors merits a condemnation, by law." Which is true. I replied in Arabic: "If you've been asked to kick people out, go ahead! You file your report, and I'll file mine ... I pay more homage to those who died to liberate our country than you do. I do it through my work, in the service I give to the students. The moudjahidin paid with their lives so that our children would have the right to knowledge, not so they'd be robbed of it."

At the beginning of the next term, he penalized me by giving me nothing but classes of literature students whom I had to teach in classical Arabic.[1] I refused this arbitrary measure. I decided to continue doing my classes in French, which is my way of teaching. It is not that I have a language problem, since I'm perfectly fluent in classical Arabic. But the Algerian way of making instruction all-Arabic has, in the area of mathematics, produced an unacceptable

---

1. See "Language in Algeria" in the Glossary.

modification in content—an imprecision in concepts and a lack of rigor in reasoning—as if math weren't an exact science! I explained my decision to my students, who supported me, and I sent a letter to their parents and to the inspector at the Academy. One week later, when I arrived at school in the morning, the guard stopped me and said: "You no longer belong to this establishment." Yes, it was the doorman who told me this! I went to see the inspector, who was getting tired of this business, and he said: "Go and find yourself a position, and we'll assign you to it." I had no friends in the right places, no one who could pull strings for me. Then I got the idea of going back to my old high school, Hassiba Ben-Bouali. The principal welcomed me with open arms, and I started that very day. But she warned me: "Be careful, Khalida! The number of bilingual classes is going down every year. You'll have to be ready to teach some classes in Arabic." And that's what I did as of the following term, when I had to teach one course in Arabic and found that I was very uneasy teaching the math in the syllabus in that language, whose intellectual rigor was beginning to disappear.

In 1989, all the classes at the high school were, indeed, Arabized. Because I didn't want to change my profession, I asked to be assigned to the French Lycée Descartes, formerly known as Fromentin, which was the high school you attended, Elisabeth. It had just been nationalized, but a part of the school remained bilingual, and they needed teachers. As you know, it's a school that has always had excellent standards, with an outstanding success rate on the baccalauréat. In that sense, I was happy there. But in the other part of the high school the damage done by Arabization was terribly evident. They killed philosophy, they killed Darwin, and they eliminated all the texts that sharpen the critical faculties. I was furious to see that the syllabi and the quality of my section were not offered to all young Algerians. What right did the leaders of the nation have to decide that this segment of Algeria's youth weren't worthy of that, when they themselves chose the bilingual classes for their own children? How could anyone avoid drawing the conclusion that, for those who were governing us, Arabization was a method of total social control, an instrument for alienating the people, while the leaders ensured that an elite would be reproduced for their own benefit?

E.S.: After a few years, therefore, the devastating effects of the reform Chadli* had initiated in 1980 became apparent. Chadli's reform program formally established what Boumediene* had set in motion. From that point on, from primary school to the end of a student's university career, French—the language of an ex-occupier who was still held in contempt, and a language now held hostage by the stormy relations between France and Algeria—was forsaken. Furthermore, the content of what was being taught was bound to produce fundamentalists. Can you give some precise examples of this shift?

K.M.: I'll tell you an anecdote concerning primary school, which was entirely dominated by the Koran. It was the son of a woman friend of mine who told us this. His teacher asked all the students to bring in a cork stopper, in order to do a practical experiment. The next day, only a fraction of the children, including this little boy, had that object in their possession. Why? Because, in our country, cork stoppers are used only in wine bottles, and many Algerians don't drink alcohol. The children who had their corks were very proud. But there wasn't going to be any experiment! It was a trap. The teacher terrorized the "guilty" children by launching into a violent diatribe against their miscreant parents who didn't obey *charia**. He explained that it was up to them to enforce the law of God; otherwise they would go to hell, where Satan was waiting for them. He added that if their mothers didn't wear the veil, they would be hung by their hair, and so on. I know hundreds of stories like this one.

To give an example of what happened at the secondary school level, I think it's interesting to leaf through the Arabic literature and reading textbook for the ninth grade. This is a "reflective" book designed by the state. Chapter 2: "The Koran and the *Hadiths**"; chapter 3: "The Art of Speaking According to an Ancestor of the Prophet, the Prophet, and Ben Badis*"; chapter 4: "The Art of Advice, by a Woman to Her Daughter Who Is Preparing to Be Married" (or, how to become the slave of a man); chapter 5: "On the Charter of War, According to the First Inspired Caliph, Abou bakr Essedik"; chapter 6: "The Proverbs and Wise Words, a Text by the Imam Ali"; and finally, to represent all the rich and magnificent poetry that has been written in Arabic ... three poems, including one by the Emir Abd el-Kader, who is obviously not acknowledged as having been a freemason! What can come out of all of that?

E.S.: Did you yourself experience manifestations of fundamentalism? How did you react, now that you held the authority of a schoolteacher?

K.M.: I found the first evidence, I think, in a student's paper that began with "All powerful and merciful God" and ended with "It is God who is responsible for my success or failure." Then there was a boy in his senior year who never looked me in the face when I asked him a question, who always had his eyes lowered. I learned through some colleagues that he was a fundamentalist who was hostile to co-ed classes. One day he asked to speak to me at the end of class "because there was a problem." Then he told me: "Ma'am, we like you a lot, and we respect you as we do our mothers, our sisters ..." I already knew what he was getting at, but I played dumb: "What's wrong? Am I going too fast in class? Or is it that I speak in French, and you can't manage to keep up?" "No, no, it's not that at all! It's simply that you're missing something ..." "Ah, and what might that be?" "You know, Ma'am, you're young, and we are too, and when there are men and women in the same place ..." With his eyes still lowered, he added "there's Satan, and you're missing the *sotra* to protect us from Satan playing tricks on us." "Sotra" is a very strong term, which literally means "to veil." In short, he was asking me to put on a *hidjab**. I discussed this with him at great length and cautioned him, very nicely: "What matters between you and me, in class, is that you get ready for your baccalauréat exam. If I fail in my duty as a teacher to ensure that you succeed, you'll have the right to complain. As for the rest, you should know that I'll never wear a hidjab. That being said, you're free to come to class or not." He disappeared for a week. I was worried, because my responsibility as a teacher was to avoid excluding him, at all costs. I knew what sort of life he lived. We were in a very working-class neighborhood, and this boy lived in an apartment complex near the high school, with his whole family. They had eleven children in a two-room apartment. He had no place to work, other than the mosque, which was a hundred meters from his home and which was run by fundamentalists. They had opened study halls there, and introduced review classes. I myself gave remedial classes in my spare time, precisely to help students like these. The "Barbus" ["Bearded Ones"] may even have thought that I was competing with them. Every day, this young man heard political sermons. When you consider all that, it seems inevitable that he became a fundamentalist! To make a long story short, I spoke about this matter with two of his friends, and they confessed that the boy was ashamed of his attitude but didn't know how to return to school. They finally convinced him that I would gladly take him back, with no hard feelings. And when he came back, I had him go to the blackboard, taking care to give him some very easy exercises to do, just to show him that the matter was closed.

E.S.: What happened to him?

K.M.: He spent the rest of the year with his eyes lowered, and he did well on his baccalauréat exam ... In 1992, as I was going to see an aunt who was sick in the hospital, I heard someone calling me. I turned and saw a tall, handsome young man in a white coat. It was my former student. He was a doctor, in his first year as a specialist. I had already had some problems with the fundamentalists, and he had seen me during a televised debate in which I had faced off with Abassi Madani*. He wanted to lend me his support.

E.S.: This example speaks in favor of tolerance ...

K.M.: It would be too simple to interpret it that way, and very dangerous! Let's say that, during the period when fundamentalism was beginning to take hold, as is the case today in the suburbs of France, the firmness I showed in standing up to this boy forced him to make a choice. Without that, he probably would have stayed on the same path. In fact, he wasn't a militant deep down, and he wanted to pull himself up through his studies, which I placed above everything else by publicly proselytizing in favor of school. I think my double determination allowed him to make a real choice. I'm convinced that this is the only attitude to assume, when there is still time. Afterward, when the government's weakness—which it tried to pass off as high-mindedness—opened the way for fundamentalism, no one could fight the tide any longer.

E.S.: Can you cite other examples of fundamentalism?

K.M.: Oh, yes! Here's one of a different nature, but which happened during the same period. Every morning, in one of my classes, I would find a swastika drawn on the blackboard ... I told you that I had found out about the Holocaust during my first stay in France, in 1979. From the distress I felt at this discovery, I reached a few conclusions. The first was that a school which does-n't teach the genocide of the Jews by the Nazis in its history classes, and which doesn't make this one of the components of humanity's collective memory, can't produce democratic citizens. Unless one knows about the sacred value of liberty, and about its opposite, totalitarianism, one cannot be a responsible thinker. In short, seeing this swastika every day made me hopping mad. I couldn't figure out who was doing it. I announced to the class that I would go on strike until that person came forward. And that's what I did. During the next class, the student in question confessed but said that he was not going to stop. I threw him out of class, warning him that he couldn't return until he had agreed not to put this swastika on the board any more. He ended up coming back, several days later. I made a stern speech on authority, and I decided to talk about the swastika, Nazism, and the Jews. After all, if I was going to militate for freedom, I was duty bound to teach about genocide! I asked this student: "Do you know what this kind of cross means?" He was pretty much ignorant of everything. By pressing him, I learned that a colleague of mine, who taught history and geography, had told the students that Hitler was a great guy because he had killed the Jews and was on his way to killing all the Westerners who were nonbelievers, communists, freemasons, and so on. Of course, this teacher had told them this in Arabic. So I, too, said what I had to say in Arabic. And I emphasized what I believed at the time: that the Arabs, being Semites, were bound to suffer the same fate as the Jews. In fact, I was terrified for their future and the future of our country. These students were barely five or six years younger than I was: how, in such a short time, had the Algerian school system created such zombies, with such weak, manipulable, violent, and hateful minds, ready to swallow all sorts of rubbish? This was the result of a history program that was three-quarters devoted to the Middle East, and of an almost daily bombardment by the television, which presented the Israeli-Palestinian conflict in an exclusively anti-Jewish light.

E.S.: It's clear from your tale that young people were being influenced both by their mosques and by teachers who were already converted to fundamentalism. Just how indoctrinated were teachers, at this point in time?

K.M.: There's nothing better than a personal anecdote to take the measure of that ... In this incident, a woman colleague from my high school invited me to an exhibit—exhibits were only allowed if the head of the school authorized it. What was the theme? "The Muslim Book and the Hidjab." I went, and I saw, next to the Koran, an entire collection of cheap books printed in Algeria, in some cases, but mostly in the Middle East. It was all drivel used throughout the Muslim world, which told girls about their duty to stay pure, about submission, and about how to put on the head scarf ... All this circulated freely while Kateb Yacine* was banned by the F.L.N. and the Islamists, and while anti-establishment Arabic-language writers like Ouacini Laaredj* produced manuscripts that were rotting in the desk drawers of the censors! I told this teacher in Arabic: "You don't have the right to do this at school!" "Why not? We're educating the students along the lines of their religion, so that they'll be shaped by it." "This isn't religion, it's a fundamentalist ideology." "Ah, you're afraid, right? You're afraid that people will become Muslims!" "We're already Muslims! I'm afraid that, because of you, they'll become fundamentalists!" It was clear that the high school administration had given the green light for this exhibit. The problem was that the administration did the same thing in most schools, out of cowardice or ideological complicity. The teachers who, in reaction, wanted to organize exhibits on cultural topics couldn't do so.

E.S.: Let's talk in detail about the hidjab, which preoccupies so many teachers in France today.

K.M.: In 1987 there still weren't very many girls wearing them in my classes, never more than five out of an average of forty-two students. During the following school term, I was shocked to see that half the girls were wearing the hidjab. I tried to downplay the situation, telling myself that these were students going through a classic identity crisis. I was well aware that, in this same high school that had made me what I am, I was the one who had become a stranger. These girls in their hidjabs corresponded to the Algerian school system, to what the government and the fundamentalists wanted to do with Algerian society. It scared me very much. It's painful, you know, to consider the full implications of such a realization. Soon thereafter, I wrote an article in which I explained that "not all hidjabs are Islamist." I advanced the idea that a woman was hidden behind every hidjab. I still think that. I continue to believe that there are multiple reasons for wearing one: to be left in peace in the street or the workplace, to show one's religious conviction, to be coquettish, to hide one's poverty, or because one has yielded to familial and social pressure. I also spoke in that article about the political hidjab, which is the sign that one subscribes to a totalitarian religious ideology, a uniform that is quickly transformed into a shroud for women. But I still couldn't see at that time that this kind of hidjab was going to crush all the others and become a weapon, the "emblem" of the G.I.A.*

E.S.: So, you did nothing to fight it?

K.M.: In my classes, no. That's a hard thing to admit, but I have to be honest. As with the Iranian revolution, I didn't make the connection between this and everything that was happening, this time in my own country. I had an unconscious wish to take part in the general, willing blindness. I can only come up with one explanation for this: like many teachers and militants of my generation, I was, at the time, convinced that rationality would ultimately triumph. It seemed impossible to me that things might turn out differently.

E.S.: Even so, that's extraordinary! For, during the same period, you were aware that Islamic institutes, baccalauréat exams, and universities had great seductive powers ...

K.M.: That's true. But I understand why they were seductive. The "diplomas" those establishments awarded gave people access to anything and everything. They thus opened the doors to social mobility, to changes in status. That is more attractive than knowledge for many people. At the time, however, I thought this wouldn't have any consequences for the bulk of the population, that it primarily affected rural areas and wouldn't spread to the cities. That was wrong, I admit!

E.S.: In fact, you long persisted in seeing things through the logic of a democrat who was simply fighting against the dictatorship. That is how you came to be a member of the Algerian League for Human Rights as soon as it was created in 1985.

K.M.: Because I am a feminist, I was, in fact, contacted by a group that wanted to create this League. It included militants from the Berber cultural movement, Trotskyists, and lawyers such as Ali Yahya*. It was on this occasion that I met Saïd Sadi* for the first time.

Saïd is the pride and joy of my generation. He enjoys an exceptional legitimacy. He's a few years older than we are, but he doesn't belong to the generation of the war of liberation, either. He organized the Berber uprising of 1980, and was the first man who dared to defy the government, paid for it, but persisted in spite of everything. For me, he's the great leader. Thus, on March 15, 1985, the Algerian League for Human Rights saw the light of day. To tell the truth, I was following things from a distance, because I had just suffered a personal tragedy: I had given birth to a little girl who'd died from a birth defect. So I was a bit surprised when Saïd, with his troops, and Ali Yahya walked out in a huff shortly afterward and founded a different league ... with Ali Yahya as its president. This league was much harder and combative than mine was, in fact. Moreover, all its members were arrested in July and August. Some of them, including Saïd and the singer Ferhat, were gruesomely tortured in the Lambèse penitentiary. The state security court condemned them to prison, after a joke of a trial. Chadli pardoned them in 1987. So you can understand why I am scandalized today when I hear certain people say that the democrats didn't rise up against the F.L.N. That's revisionism, pure and simple!

E.S.: In 1989, disagreements arose between Saïd Sadi and Ali Yahya. That would turn out to be an important moment. Why?

K.M.: Saïd made a mistake in offering the League to Ali Yahya; for the lawyer turned against him, and then against us, when Sadi created the R.C.D.*, or Rally for Culture and Democracy, in 1989. Ali Yahya made a political choice in favor of an entirely different option: that of the Islamists. He ousted Sadi from the League, took it over, and changed its bylaws. He transformed it into a tool of the fundamentalists, and stripped it of its mission of fighting for human rights.

E.S.: Up to that point, Ali Yahya—who had been one of Boumediene's ministers—had defended all of the victims of the regime, whether they were democrats, supporters of Ben Bella*, communists, or Islamists. What proof do you have that his attitude changed?

K.M.: The first place to look for that proof is in the new bylaws he established for the League. Few people bother to read them. Here, for example, is what is said at the beginning of chapter 5, entitled "Islam and Human Rights": "Islam is not only a religion, but also a law, a culture, a community, and a social, juridical, philosophical, and economic way of life. A clear and sufficient answer must be given to the Islamic conception of human rights ..." Ali Yahya's ideological choice was made when he wrote that. Moreover, he refused, soon thereafter, to defend a woman who had been sexually assaulted by the fundamentalists, and he did so for a reason. It is common knowledge—a spokesman for the F.I.S.* confirmed this during an R.F.I. [Radio France Internationale] broadcast in April 1992—that Ali Yahya was supposed to be named Minister of Justice in the event that the Islamists won. All this would prove to have serious consequences much later. Ali Yahya was present at the Rome meeting of January 1995*, where an unacceptable platform was produced. In the eyes of the entire world, which was unaware of everything I've been telling you about, he brought the backing of a league for human rights! Given that, how could the international observers at the Rome meeting not feel reassured? But of course, during the 1980s, which was also the decade of great democratic ferment and which was to end with the uprising of October 1988, we were far from foreseeing any of that.

Chapter 8
"I'm Still Wondering About October 1988"

Elisabeth Schemla: In the summer of 1988, the noose was tightening around you. You decided to leave Algeria, at least for a while, and go to stay with your brother in the United States. Why did you reach such a decision, when you say today that exile would be the worst possible situation for you? And why did you choose America, when your cultural sphere is the Mediterranean?

Khalida Messaoudi: However extraordinary it may seem to you, I had, at that time, the feeling that there was no possibility of overcoming this Algerian regime. Paradoxically, I was much more discouraged than I am today: the situation back then didn't seem to offer any perspective, which is not the case now. I had the sense that I'd been defeated on every front, after eight years of incessant battles in which I was like an ant being crushed by the force of the dictatorship. It was the time in the wilderness for the women's movement: every attempt at initiating a popular uprising was bloodily suppressed, as had happened at Sétif and Constantine a year earlier, in 1987. I myself believed I was no longer capable of practicing my profession in a way that respected intelligence, and thought that if I continued teaching, I would be the accomplice of a system that would produce failure at best, and fundamentalism at worst. I needed to clear my head, for fear of going crazy! But it wasn't a question for me of going into exile, and I chose the United States solely because my brother had offered to take care of me, in the name of the family solidarity I have already evoked.

E.S.: In the end, you decided against leaving. Why?

K.M.: Chadli* held me back! I'll explain. At the very moment that I wanted to leave my country, in September 1988, this man made a televised speech addressed to the nation's professionals and told Algerians that they were henceforth forbidden from sending their children to a French high school, saying literally: "Those who disagree with us can take their suitcases and leave the country!" I was indignant, like the vast majority of Algerians, even though most were not affected by this measure. How could a head of state, who was theoretically responsible for his people, make such a pronouncement of disdain and exclusion toward those who simply didn't think the way he did? Wasn't this already a sign of the delirious perversion—also evident among fundamentalists— that consists in branding any Algerian who opposed the system a foreigner in his own land? By using the term "us," wasn't Chadli admitting publicly that the F.L.N.* considered Algeria to be its private property? After this declaration of war, which included equal measures of stupidity and arrogance, it would have been shameful to leave the field clear to this "gang." If anyone had to go, it was precisely Chadli and his people, who had led the country to ruin! My determination to stay was, of course, reinforced a few weeks later by the great hope that arose from the popular uprisings of October.

E.S.: Did you feel anything in the air that already hinted at the coming rebellion?

K.M.: People were getting fed up with shortages of all sorts: everything was lacking, housing, coffee, sugar, semolina, soap, and even black pepper, which is one of the major spices in our cuisine. Everything had begun to be overpriced when the price of gasoline fell in 1986, and discontent was flourishing everywhere. In the halls of power, the confrontations between those who wanted to liberalize the economy and privatize, and those who adhered stubbornly to central planning, were becoming violent. These confrontations showed clearly in the speeches of Chadli, who belonged to the first camp. The government's projects for industrial restructuring, which threatened to cost a good number of jobs, triggered strikes in every region. In Algiers, the port was blocked and shut down by the dockers from the factories. Most important, from September to early October, although it had mobilized all its means of repression, the regime could not manage either to control or to cover up the two big union conflicts that were shaking the capital: that of the Sonacom* [National Society for Mechanical Construction], and that of the P.T.T.* In short, the social climate was obviously explosive, but no one saw a way out and no one was expecting what was about to happen.

E.S.: So were you, a militant who had taken part in so many fights, surprised by the explosion?

K.M.: You can't imagine just how surprised I was! Beginning on October 1, I heard people talking all around me, and the rumor spread like wildfire: "We have to get ready! On October 5, things are going to get hot, and everyone is going to take to the streets!" I tried in vain to find out through my militant friends if this rumor corresponded to a call for rebellion, and who had started it. No one was able to tell me. We were in the dark. And the truth is, I didn't believe this story for a minute! Despite the general ferment and tension, such an outcome seemed utterly improbable to me: how could the government allow such a thing to happen?

E.S.: So, on October 5, you went to your high school as usual ...

K.M.: During my first class, two young men—rather unexpected in a girls' school, no?—interrupted the class and asked me to excuse my students so that they could go out and demonstrate in the street. For a spontaneous demonstration, one could do better. I realized that the same approach was being used throughout the building. Where did these boys come from? From a neighboring high school, in Kouba. The administration asked us to have the students go down to the courtyard. And what did I see there? Cars, which had been rushed over by the ruling elite to pick up these girls and drive them to safety: among them were the daughters of President Chadli and of Mohamed Cherif Messaadia, the secretary general of the F.L.N.

E.S.: Did you join the stream of demonstrators?

K.M.: There was an extraordinary flood of young people, who were singing, chanting slogans, and dancing: I was amazed, fascinated. But I felt old and stupid ...! My first reflex was to try to understand what they were demanding. I asked some of them a few questions. They answered: "Ma'am, this is it, this is liberty!" I decided to go to some other neighborhoods in Algiers to see how big the uprising was. Everywhere, the streets were teeming with people. From that very first day, the destruction began; for all these young people, who were primarily high school students or unemployed, weren't content to shout out in hatred against the regime and its men, they wanted to attack and destroy everything that represented the state and the F.L.N.: the seat of the party cells, the town halls, the police stations, the army's research centers, the offices of Air Algérie, the state stores, and the Ministries of Youth and Sports, of National Education, and of Professional Training. The fire of the rebellion spread through all the big cities in the country. It all lasted for a good week, under the state of siege and the cease-fire that Chadli had decreed on the second day of the riots. The government's response was ferocious. There were thousands of arrests, torturing, and soldiers firing on the demonstrators with automatic rifles. Doctors estimated that five hundred people were killed and thousands wounded.

E.S: What exactly were these young people demanding? Democracy, as the Chinese students in Tienanmen Square demanded a year later?

K.M.: No, they never called for democracy in any of their slogans. And they never called for an Islamic state, either. It's very important to emphasize that no fraction of the opposition predicted this event. The young people's only demand, which they hammered home in a variety of ways, was this: dignity and justice, and pride in being themselves. As one slogan put it, "Ma neshakouch felfel ekhel neshakou Raïs Fhel": "We don't need black pepper, we need a decent leader."* Moreover, in these riots, where young people were seen drinking beer, singing, and dancing in one street of Algiers, there was an explosion of life that had been repressed for too long, a sort of liberating joy, a healthy collective catharsis that was good for them but especially for us, who had forgotten how to live. Those of us in the older generation had memorized the doctrine of the revolutionaries or that of the Islamists, but we were missing the point. I wasn't bothered by the image of myself that was reflected back by these young people. In my eyes, they showed me tremendous generosity: they gave me their strength, the strength to carry on. What was intolerable was to see them, without any organization or real spokespeople, getting themselves massacred.

E.S.: What did you, in the organized opposition, do during this uprising which took you by surprise?

K.M.: We tried to stay close to this movement, which surpassed us, in fact, but which we supported wholeheartedly. However, the members of the youth movement were creating an incomprehensible jumble that equated the state with the men who embodied it and the buildings that represented it. Obviously, we thought that there was an important difference. So we promptly drew up several initiatives that corresponded to our idea of action, but which, unfortunately, were not centralized. Some teachers, including myself, tried to establish a committee to organize these young people somewhat, at least those to whom we were close as teachers. We spent our time in endless meetings where we debated this, grappling with our democratic scruples: it was crucial that we avoid taking things over from the real rebels or betraying their demands, which were not easy to translate into a negotiable platform. During this time, seventy Algerian journalists published a declaration in which they denounced the ban on reporting and condemned the lack of respect for freedom of the press, the violence of repression, arbitrary arrests, torture, and the entire political system. They demanded that all the democratic liberties be recognized. In Kabylia*, a general strike succeeded wonderfully. Texts calling for democracy streamed forth. The student movement in Algiers merged with the youth movement, organized meetings everywhere, and also demanded democracy. The Algerian League for Human Rights, led by Miloud Brahimi, began a remarkable effort to counter torture: they collected testimony and put together files—which mysteriously disappeared from the League headquarters a short time later. And then, an event that had no precedent in Algerian history occurred ...

E.S.: What event?

K.M.: The formation of a National Committee Against Torture.

E.S.: Who initiated that?

K.M.: Doctors were the principal driving force behind the creation of this committee, because they were the best witnesses to the horror. The great pediatrician Djilali Belkhenchir, the psychiatrist Mahfoud Boucebci, and the independent film director Jean-Pierre Lledo were the three key figures. There were also some college professors, jurists—including Ali Yahya*—artists, journalists, and militant women. Many committee members were communists, like my old philosophy teacher, Rabah Guenzet, who kept me regularly informed so that I could in turn report on what was happening during the meetings I attended. This committee succeeded in eliciting public testimony from the largely apolitical members of the youth movement and from communists, the latter of whom paid dearly for it. They had all come straight from the hands of their torturers. I heard unbearable stories and saw for myself the scars of torture: fingernails torn out, genitals mutilated, the aftereffects of being sodomized with glass bottles or clubs, or being subjected to electric shock, water torture ... For the first time, the hideous face of this abject government, which had been hidden for thirty-six years with the full complicity of the leaders of the Western nations, was at last brought to light and exposed to the entire world. You can't begin to know how grateful I am toward this committee. The work it did was a decisive gain for Algeria. The Black Book it produced is a hefty, irrefutable, indisputable document.

I should add that at no time did the Islamists attempt to create a committee against torture; never did we hear them utter a single word of protest against these barbarous practices! How can anyone help seeing a connection between their attitude and the fact that, a short time later, they would in turn begin persecuting and torturing people? How can one fail to point out that among their victims were Belkhenchir, Boucebci and Guenzet, who were all assassinated by the F.I.S.* by being shot or stabbed to death? Finally, how can we forget that Anwar Haddam, the F.I.S. representative in Washington and one of the people who signed the Rome platform in January 1995*, claimed responsibility for the murder of Boucebci on television and described it as "the execution of a legal sentence"?

E.S.: While the various sectors of the opposition were working to ensure that the October rebellion led to greater democratization, the Islamists were following a very different strategy ...

K.M.: They had been militarily dismantled ever since the time when Bouyali and his Algerian Islamic Movement [M.I.A.*] were being hunted down, which lasted from 1982 to 1987. Like us, they were caught unawares. But the uprising soon revealed their own strategic divergences. The day after October 5, old Ahmed Sahnoune, who was president of the Algerian Islamic *Daâwa** and who was opposed to armed violence, made public a communiqué that had been written in his mosque and distributed throughout the working-class neighborhoods of Algiers. Following the example of the democratic, secular trend, he explained the upheaval as stemming from the bankruptcy of the system. But he asked "all Muslim citizens" to go home, citing the *hadith**: "They are destroying their houses with their own hands." As a solution to the crisis, he proposed that Algerians "return to Islam as *charia** and as a methodology after the failure of the corrupting regimes."[1] He was not followed by the young people, who continued to fight. Above all, he was thwarted by another wing of the Islamist movement, since an "anonymous" call was issued to hold a huge demonstration instead. This call came, in fact, from Ali Benhadj*, who was discreetly supported by Abassi Madani*, and it was an undeniably successful mobilization effort.

E.S.: Was Benhadj an unknown figure at the time?

K.M.: I don't think so, given that the Islamists had at their disposal the network of mosques I've told you about. For example, I was working in Kouba at the time and could hear his sermons over the loudspeakers of the mosque. The people of Bab el-Oued also listened to him: the Sounna mosque was his favorite.

E.S.: How did you discover that there were negotiations underway between the government, which had its back to the wall, and the Islamists?

K.M.: I realized this because, in a one-party regime, a man like Sahnoune who puts his name to a communiqué every day, can only do so if he is guaranteed impunity. Simply put, we eventually found out that he had been received at the presidential mansion. In fact, Chadli chose him, and him alone, to serve as a go-between with the government, and thus as the representative of the youth movement! ... Why didn't Chadli select a group of young demonstrators, or union workers, for example? Is it because he had decided, unilaterally, that Algerian youth had to be represented by the fundamentalists?

E.S.: However, one of the Islamists' demonstrations also ended bloodily, in Bab el-Oued ...

K.M.: I think the government, with the complicity of Ali Benhadj, deliberately provoked what remained of that crowd of fundamentalist demonstrators in order to show them and all the

---

1. See Aïssa Khelladi, *Algérie: Les Islamistes face au pouvoir* (Alger: Editions Alfa, 1992).

other groups who were there that it was ready to resort to any type of slaughter to quell an uprising. The army did the same thing two days later in Kabylia, in Tizi-Ouzou, because Chadli wanted to show that the streets were his. Moreover, he made a speech in which he took personal responsibility for the repression. He also announced some reforms that were on the way: a referendum on a new Constitution that would allow for a certain pluralism, and a "redistribution" of the executive and legislative powers.

E.S.: Was this the first time during October 1988 that you had to face the Algerian army? How did you react?

K.M.: For us, October 1988 was like undergoing psychoanalysis. It forced us to open our eyes. The army had been in power for twenty-six years, without any legitimacy. But, in our collective unconscious, it was a fact that we had more or less openly accepted since 1962. Why? Because this army, which was born out of the glorious A.L.N.*, had liberated the country and tried to ease all the pains of colonization; it seemed normal to us, after that, that the army should run the country. That may seem extraordinary, particularly on the part of opposition members, but that's the way it was. At school, for example, I'd been taught in great detail that the army serves the people, not repression. So, when I saw the tanks, the armored cars, and the uniformed soldiers in the street, and then saw everything that ensued, I was immediately reminded of Bigeard and Massu.* It was an unavoidable, compelling image. I realized that the army of my country was just like the one it had fought, the colonial army. It was a shock. I had an overwhelming feeling of revolt, of injustice. Nothing was worse than this discovery: the colonels of my country destroyed a myth when they showed that they were capable of firing on unarmed Algerians! I couldn't accept that they would strip us so suddenly of our only remaining source of pride in being Algerians. The war of liberation was the only thing that held us together as a nation, and during those days, these criminals killed us twice. From that point of view, too, October 1988 was historic.

E.S.: Wasn't it also the beginning of the divorce between the army and the F.L.N.?

K.M.: It was the beginning of the army's repudiation of the F.L.N.! The husband discovered that his wife was too unpopular, so he started getting rid of her, little by little.

E.Ś.: Was all that staged, in your view? And by whom?

K.M.: In the end, that question doesn't seem very important. Even if we suppose that events were being manipulated by the Chadli clan, which supported the economic liberalism it was trying to impose, the fact remains that this clan was completely over-taken by events. It may have expected a stick of dynamite, but it got a powder keg. Nonetheless, if we add things up objectively in hindsight, we can clearly see who were the losers in the regime: the proponents of state-run industry and economic stagnancy—that is, Chadli's adversaries. And who were the winners? Another clan from the same regime. But all that is just a hypothesis, given that we were lacking the transparency of a democratic government.

Chapter 9
A Bomb in Algeria: The F.I.S.

Elisabeth Schemla: After the October 1998 outburst, Chadli*
and the F.L.N.* undertook a "controlled easing of restrictions."
This triggered an effervescence of democratic activity. The Constitution, which was approved by a referendum, made the government responsible to the Parliament and omitted all reference to
the F.L.N. and to socialism. Chadli, who had just been reelected as
president of the Republic, committed himself to the creation of a
Union of Arabian Maghreb that also included Morocco, Maurita-
nia, Tunisia, and Libya. A great number of associations, including
your own, were finally recognized. The path was opening to a mul-
tiparty government ...

Khalida Messaoudi: I watched all this through the perspective of
a feminist, first and foremost. And what did I see? First of all, I saw
that this "democratization" was occurring while the Family Code*
was still in place, and that there was no question of repealing that
code. Second, I saw that a law on political parties, which I supported, and which made it illegal to found a party on a religious,
regional, or sexist basis, had no sooner passed than the government itself flouted it by legalizing religious parties, notably the
F.I.S.*, on September 14, 1989! Finally, I saw that the electoral law
adopted for the municipal elections that were to be held in June
1990 authorized a husband to vote for his wife. From my point of
view, women were once again going to be sacrificed, and I could
not accept that. What was new was that our association was, in fact,
recognized, and that the liberalization of the press, the radio, and
television gave me access to an audience I had not been allowed to
reach before. But, frankly, the year 1989 was a special turning
point for me because I became conscious—at last—of the danger

posed by the Islamic Salvation Front [F.I.S.]. Even if I still used the term "acts of intolerance" to describe the horrors this group was now committing in full public view, I understood what a threat it was.

E.S.: At what point, exactly?

K.M.: When, in June 1989, a fundamentalist commando set fire to the house of a woman from Ouargla simply because she lived alone with her seven children and was thus, in the eyes of these madmen, a "prostitute," a danger to the community, or *oumma*, and a source of discord, or *fitna*. One of her sons was burned to death. This tragedy had the effect of a bomb in Algerian society. During that summer, this type of act became more and more frequent, and a nurse was burned alive by her fundamentalist brother because she had too much contact with men at work.

E.S.: So what did your association do to promote equal rights between men and women?

K.M.: All the feminist organizations, which were proliferating, mobilized and demanded that the government guarantee women's safety. In my group, however, the discussions that took place on the subject of this demand were quite heated. We had some Trotskyists in our ranks: they felt that by demanding protection we were, in fact, calling for repression. The arguments we had were fierce, and they only got worse over the course of 1989. The core of the problem was that we didn't see the increasingly violent F.I.S. in at all the same light. Women were subject to more and more punitive strikes, particularly those who lived alone or who refused to wear the *hidjab** in the workplace. The harassment was constant. An F.I.S. tract on women made this declaration: "Mother, sister, wife, as your father, brother, husband, I would like your beauty to be my wealth, for I cannot live without you. I seethe with jealousy when I see you working as a secretary for a human fox who asked for your photo before he hired you. I don't want you to be a work tool, or a scapegoat for those who seek to destroy Islamic morals ..." In another passage, it said: "I don't want you to use the Jewish word 'emancipation' to attack the Islamic values of your ancestors and make the feminist organizations happy." Under these conditions, which I found unacceptable, it was natural for a crisis to occur in my association. I was a president who could no longer get any consensus.

E.S.: Were you hoping the group would split in two?

K.M.: Yes, because there was a fundamental debate involved. I could not longer accept the argument that the F.I.S. was a popular revolutionary movement fighting a corrupt bourgeois government, because those who espoused it skirted the issue of the F.I.S.'s ideology, its project for an Islamic state, and its methods. During the last debate we had between the two factions in our organization, in January 1990, one of the Trotskyists said to me: "Ali Benhadj* is in favor of not paying back debts [Algeria's debt to Western banks], so you can clearly see that he is on the people's side!" At that point, I resigned and, along with all the friends who followed me, I founded another movement, the Association Indépendante pour le Triomphe des Droits des Femmes [Independent Association for the Triumph of Women's Rights].

E.S.: Your entire philosophy is expressed in the adjective "independent" that you included in the acronym A.I.T.D.F.*

K.M.: Ever since I moved away from the communists at the age of twenty-one and got involved in the struggle for women's rights, I have refused to subordinate the question of women to a party. And that is more true today than ever. When women act as militants within political organizations, they too often keep quiet about their own demands, which is heartbreaking but classic. I don't reproach them for this, and I don't think they're being manipulated by men, but I don't subscribe to their choice. In early 1989, we went to see the communist women militants, who had just formed an association, to suggest that we work together; but they told us: "That's impossible, because our objectives are not the same. We don't want the Family Code to be repealed, we want it amended. The people are not ready for egalitarian civil rights; we have to keep in mind their religious sentiments, and reform things from the inside." It's always the same story ... With the Trotskyists in my association, I had the feeling, once again, that we were the echo chamber for a party. I want women to speak autonomously, especially in a group like ours. That's what I call freedom. Unfortunately, many of the women who are involved in political organizations do not grant other women this right of sovereignty.

E.S.: Louisa Hannoun* was one of the Trotskyists in your association. She would later turn up in Rome in January 1995*, during the negotiations with the fundamentalists. Her party was not a major player on the Algerian political scene, but she brought a "feminist" backing to that platform which reassured the international observers. Do you view her participation in those negotiations as the natural culmination of an ideological stance that you had already challenged?

K.M.: I have nothing to say about Louisa Hannoun.

E.S.: You speak of independence. But you yourself are so close to the R.C.D.*, or Rally for Culture and Democracy, which Saïd Sadi* founded in 1989, that it's hard to avoid seeing you as a major player and go-between for this party from the time of its inception.

K.M.: You're free to think that, but I disagree with your assessment. I have never been a member of the R.C.D.; even though I'm sympathetic to its cause, that doesn't make me its spy. At the beginning, I was invited to its meetings as a feminist. I've already told you how much I admire Saïd. Most of the leaders of this party are my personal friends. What we have in common is that we belong to the same generation, whose importance I've already underscored, and share the same goals for society: the separation of church and state, secularism, citizenship, a state based on rights, the repeal of the Family Code, the recognition of Algeria's Berber dimension, social justice, educational reform, and so on. I will say that, given that the R.C.D. was the first and only Algerian political party to make a public issue of the problem of secularism, which is one of my credos, it would be pretty odd for me not to feel close to this party! However, I repeat that, although I believe it's very important for women to get involved in political parties, I think it's equally important for them to have a movement that specifically addresses their identity as women. The independence I claim does not, in my mind, signify an anti-party ostracism. I am not opposed to working with parties—that's what I do with the R.C.D.—but I defend the right of women to be free in choosing their allies and naming their enemies, in function of women's interests alone. That is the heart of my involvement in Algeria, and if one fails to understand that fully, all my activities become inexplicable and meaningless. The "woman" question, and the quest for an egalitarian, secular republic, prevail over all the other components of my identity. I am a woman before I am an Algerian, a Berber, a Mediterranean, a Muslim, or a combatant ...

E.S.: Some people claim that this is a disguised form of misogyny toward Muslim women ...

K.M.: What sort of question is that? Do you mean to say that Jews, blacks, farmers, or homosexuals (for example) who are concerned about the status of Jews, blacks, farmers, or homosexuals are anti-Semitic, racist, anti-farmer, or sexist? What a joke ... or what a disgrace! If they weren't there, which one of those causes would have made any progress?

E.S.: Was it because of feminism that you didn't join Aït Ahmed* when he returned to Algeria after twenty-seven years of exile, and after his party, the F.F.S.*, was finally recognized?

K.M.: Aït Ahmed had condemned the Family Code while he was in exile in Switzerland. When he returned to Algeria, as you can imagine given what I've told you about him, I viewed the event as the return of the Messiah. Politically, I felt close to him. I was one of the thousands of people who went to greet him at the airport, and I left a conference that the R.C.D. was holding to do that. I didn't see anything contradictory in my attitude. In my mind, Aït Ahmed was coming back to lead the fight for democracy. I knew that, before his return, emissaries had proposed that he come back "for Algeria, and not just for the F.F.S." I was initially a bit surprised when, in his first speech, he announced that he had returned to serve as the secretary general of his party. But, after all, that was his right. Then I went to see him in my capacity as president of a feminist association. I was extremely moved. Before I'd even had the chance to ask him anything, he told me: "Some people reproach me for coming back to serve the F.F.S. ... I'm sure that they're denigrating me in order to break it up..." That left me speechless, because, being acquainted with certain of the people who had said that to him, I was sure that they had no ulterior motive. Then he asked me about my new association. But I quickly realized, from the tenor of his questions, that he had already met with all the other feminists and that he had adopted the viewpoint of the Trotskyists. According to them, I was working for the government and the R.C.D.!

E.S.: During this time, some people were also claiming that the R.C.D. was a product of the government; they even went so far as to claim that the government was financing it. That thesis recently reappeared in one of the articles that has been written on Algeria and published under the aegis of "Reporters Without Borders."

K.M.: To break up a party, totalitarians have always resorted to Stalinist tactics like casting doubts on its financial sources. And, to destroy a protestor or dissident, they depict the person as an agent of Military Security or smear his or her private life by saying things like "She's sleeping with cops." There's nothing more lethal, in a country run by a single party, than allowing rumors of that sort to circulate. What can I say, other than the cowards who always stab you in the back are themselves using the vile methods of Military Security, and that it all demonstrates that they're completely incapable of debating on the field of ideas? It's pathetic, and I'll repeat just once more what I said at the beginning of this interview: I refuse to fall into that trap.

E.S.: Let's go back to Aït Ahmed. What other reasons prompted you to keep your distance from him?

K.M.: I really diverged from him over the question of fundamentalism. The fact that the acts of terrorism were obviously being orchestrated from 1989 onward should have triggered a very strong reaction on his part. He, however, vaguely condemned the violence, and never pronounced the name of the group that was behind it: the F.I.S. I realized that something wasn't right. I began to move away from him. But the full break occurred, of course, at the end of 1991: it was then that there was a total and definitive split in the positions taken by the F.F.S. versus the R.C.D. and all the proponents of civil society concerning the electoral process that brought the F.I.S. to power.

E.S.: At the end of 1989, and during the first half of 1990, the F.I.S. was mobilizing more and more in the streets of Algeria. Among other things, tens of thousands of women in hidjabs marched to demand that *charia** be applied. This strengthened the camp of those who called the F.I.S. a populist movement and argued that the wishes of these Islamist women should be democratically respected. How did you react when you saw that march, and what was your answer, afterward, to the argument that tolerance was necessary?

K.M.: It was as if I'd been asked to be tolerant toward the women who mobilized in the service of Hitler or Mussolini simply because they were women! How could their participation in a barbarous movement—right down to the madness of producing pure Aryan children, for example—justify the totalitarian project? They were fully responsible as individuals. Did you know, by the way, that many of those women who marched in 1989 were teachers, professors, government workers, or other working women? They were demonstrating because they wanted to. A good number of them were true militants—they weren't a mindless herd. It's precisely on that point that I am questioned: people assert that these women must have gotten something out of their involvement. But what did they get out of it? And why? How did they come to embrace Islamism? How could they have been swayed by the text I'm about to read to you? These are excerpts from a "platform" the F.I.S. published in March 1989, at a time when this movement didn't have any program as such, apart from lifting income taxes, which is a "must" for all fascists. Here is what it says: "Islam is a global substitute for all ideological, political, economic, and social problems [. . .] Only faith in God can allow us to escape the vicious cycle of underdevelopment and the various forms of neocolonialism [. . .] To achieve global social reform, we will have recourse to *hisba**, considered as the legal means of organizing relations between the street, the market, the factory, the field, the administration, and the mosque [. . .] Hisba will also be a means of policing morals [. . .] Legislation must submit to the imperatives of charia. Hasn't the Almighty said that 'the cult of anyone who seeks a religion outside of Islam is not accepted'? Who is a better judge than God toward a people who believes firmly? [. . .] We must review the educative [*sic*] content to eliminate all the ideologies and concepts that express values contrary to Islamic values [. . .] and prevent intellectual and cultural invasion ..." Yes, I ask myself the same question: how and why do such aberrations convince women, who must realize what they signify for them and for their children?

E.S.: I know you've thought about that, Khalida, and we'll get back to it very soon ... Despite the acts of violence, and the project they had announced, the first big swing to the fundamentalists occurred in 1990, when the F.I.S. won the municipal elections of June 12. The F.I.S. swept virtually all the large Algerian cities and, of course, its "capital," Constantine. How do you explain this victory? What repercussions did you fear it would have for women?

K.M.: It was a shock, of course. I viewed it as one of the injustices of history. We had paid very dearly in the precious fight for democracy we'd been waging for more than a decade, and it was the "Barbus" ["Bearded Ones"] who were reaping the benefits. They were the ones who were benefiting from the beginnings of freedom. But I also interpreted this victory as a sign of how enormously fed up Algerians were with the F.L.N., all the more so because the F.F.S. had called for a boycott. For lack of time or preparation, since they had barely been created or legalized, the other democratic parties didn't do well in the balloting. On the other hand, I could see that Mouloud Hamrouche, the man who served as leader of the government from September 1989 to June 1991, was far from being innocent in this business ...

E.S.: What do you mean by that?

K.M.: Hamrouche, a former officer of the Algerian army whom people describe today as a civilian, a protocol attaché under Boumediene*, and a member of the Political Bureau of the F.L.N., was convinced that it was possible to reform the system from the inside. But he was, objectively, one of the principal architects of the polarization between the F.L.N. and the F.I.S. that was about to occur. His view of the situation—and far too many people still share it today, even though they have the facts right under their noses—was this: the best way to fight the F.I.S. was to let the Algerian people get a real taste of fundamentalism. Later, when he was disheartened by what ensued, he went back and threw himself into the arms of the F.L.N.! To describe this behavior, a sociologist would later coin the phrase "fruitful regression," which is a regression that is always good for other people but that one wouldn't want for oneself. So, Hamrouche allowed the passage of the law I mentioned—the one that authorized a husband to vote, in a roundabout way, for his wife or wives. Then, by adopting the new *Code communal**, he granted the F.I.S. some incredible liberties: local legal deliberations could henceforth be held in mosques. The place of worship, which as we know played a major role in establishing fundamentalism, became, quite legally, the major site of the community's political life! Women, along with citizens who didn't belong to the F.I.S.—or, even worse, who opposed it—were thereby shut out of local affairs, even though they paid their taxes. This was no longer a republic of Algerians, but a republic of F.I.S. militants. We feminists sounded the alarm on this. We organized a big meeting to denounce the situation. Because we were women—in other words, the favorite target of the fundamentalists—we undoubtedly had a better sense of the deadly extravagance of these concessions.

E.S.: Events would soon prove you right ...

K.M.: The F.I.S. exploited the public funds of our town halls, the A.P.C.* [Popular Communal Assemblies], to make deals with the mafiosi. It itself was organized like a veritable underworld, sticking its hands into all sorts of trafficking, including drug trafficking. It practiced racketeering. It appropriated state funds and redistributed them to its militants, particularly those in local districts. But, in certain areas, the fundamentalist mayors did not put those funds into local services; as a result, their towns and cities will, a few years from now, be excellent breeding grounds for cholera and other viruses. More symbolically, some of these mayors replaced the slogan of the Algerian state, "By the People and for the People," which had been inscribed over the entrances to the A.P.C., with a sign saying "Islamic Commune." That is what Guemazi, the mayor of Algiers, did: he posted the sign "Islamic City Hall" on his building, for any and all to see. And, as was the case in many other city halls, Guemazi was stockpiling an impressive arsenal of weapons and medicine in the basement as a provision for the war he was anticipating. All that was dismantled later. This point is very important. In Algeria, the arming of the Islamists initially took place in mosques, covertly, during the same time that the Islamists were being trained in the martial arts. Then, when they became eligible to hold office, they used official state buildings. I underscore this because I see the same process occurring in France and its European neighbors. It's not happening on the scale of an entire country—you're obviously impervious to an Islamist takeover—but it is going on in the ghettos of your suburbs, which are like so many mini-Algerias. Unfortunately, that would be enough to destabilize your democracy very seriously, and I am afraid you're not sufficiently aware of this. You should listen to those who've lived through this painful process, and not allow yourselves to be blinded by your ardor for tolerance!

E.S.: What were the other actions of the F.I.S.?

K.M.: Immediately after they won in the municipal elections, they took on the schools, everywhere. They terrorized the principals and the children; they imposed or tried to impose the separation of the sexes; they prohibited the teaching of French, which they called the instrument of the evil former colonial power; and they banned music and dance classes, which they saw as just as diabolical as the language of Voltaire. Their militias infiltrated all the women's sports clubs to prevent girls from joining them. They closed all the conservatories: the conservatory of Algiers was transformed into a shelter for the poor. They also provided assistance to destitute families, which was a very cunning way to gain an even larger electoral base. One can see in the F.I.S. absolutely all the classic ingredients of totalitarian populist movements, including corruption. But we should note that the F.I.S. didn't take hold or establish itself very deeply among populations that had strong cultural roots, like the Touareg, the Mozabites, and the Kabyles*.

E.S.: On December 26, 1990 the Algerian deputies adopted the generalization of classical Arabic by an impressive majority, 173 votes against 8. The next day, tens of thousands of people marched in Algiers to protest this decision, in the name of democracy. That proved two things. First, that there were, indeed, two conflicting projects for society: one of them a fundamentalist project, which saw Islam as a means and an end in itself, and viewed classical Arabic as a source of identity; the other a secular project, which called for rationality, liberty, equality, and linguistic pluralism. The second thing this proved was that the F.L.N., making concession after concession to save its skin and using an assembly that had not been democratically elected, favored the cause of the Islamist project.

K.M.: We've already seen the role the F.L.N. played concerning women and schools. The generalization of classical Arabic was just a pause in the process. After that point, all the structures were in place to give the F.I.S. a very wide path toward an Islamic state. For—and this is something we've not yet discussed—the justice system, too, was Arabized. Aside from a few remarkable magistrates who did their best (when they could) to fight corruption, the granting of undeserved privileges, and the Islamist violence that occurred during major trials in the 1980s, the justice system was controlled by illiterates or corrupted officials. In a few years, the law schools became mediocre centers for professional training. Anyone could get into them, even without a baccalauréat, and a good number of "magistrates" didn't even go to law school. The competent professors were no longer teaching, and a careful analysis of the sentences handed down by the courts shows that justice was often rendered according to charia. One law, passed during Chadli's reign, allowed a person to become a judge without going to law school: all one needed was a bachelor's degree in Islamic science. It was a deplorable caricature of the general elimination of knowledge.

E.S.: And what about the conflict between the two rival projects for society?

K.M.: That expression seems both exact and inexact to me. Let's say that, during this period, one could, in fact, interpret things in such a fashion. It was possible to believe at the time that the hundred thousand demonstrators to whom you're alluding, and who represented civil society, made up a more or less homogeneous group opposed to the Islamists. However, as events soon made clear, the divergences among the "democrats" were bigger than they seemed. Neither the social project espoused by the communists nor that of the F.F.S. was exactly the same as the project envisioned by the R.C.D. The R.C.D. put forth programs, which anyone can obtain and read, that were clearly inspired by the law, institutions, the republican model, and universal values, even though they were adapted to the particularities of Algeria. The major divergences arose, first of all, from differing interpretations of the phenomenon of fundamentalism, its ties to the regime, and the strategies to follow. For the R.C.D., fundamentalism was not a product of Algerian society; rather, it was the monstrous offspring of a violation that the state institutions had committed within the school system, the state television, the justice system, and so on (as I explained earlier). The development of Islamism as a political current was, according to this view, grounded in the failure of the regime, and had grown out of the many frustrations which stemmed from that failure. From that period on, therefore, the R.C.D. could not attack the F.I.S. without attacking the entire regime that had been in place since 1962. And vice versa, since the two were intertwined.

E.S.: Let's spend some time talking about this civil society that was thirsting after democratization, during the period 1989 to 1991. How was its frame of mind influenced by journalists, singers, and satellite dishes, which allowed Algerians to pick up French television stations, among others?

K.M.: I'll speak first about the satellite dishes. They began to sprout on rooftops during this time. Some F.I.S. commandos did their utmost to destroy them, but to no avail. Thanks to these dishes, everyone could watch the news on French television, which obviously brought a breath of freedom into Algeria. In a different sense, they were a highly appreciated source of entertainment. But my view of this phenomenon is somewhat different from the one I've often heard expressed. The profusion of riches that is displayed on your T.V. screens, and the slightly licentious tone that pervades your broadcasting, didn't necessarily have positive effects. Algeria's youth is a generation that is inevitably frustrated because it has unmet emotional, sexual, and economic needs, and also faces a terrible housing problem. And, involuntarily, what it saw on French television bore witness to that frustration. This produced an extreme exasperation and exacerbated hatred in our young people, both toward themselves and toward the impious foreigners who seemed to have everything. But don't misunderstand me: I am obviously not a supporter of the F.I.S. militias! I don't want to ban satellite dishes! I simply want to emphasize that it is urgently important to get rid of this government so that we can undertake the serious reforms that will help our young people to make a truly better life for themselves.

E.S.: What did journalists contribute?

K.M.: Quite a bit, and Algerian journalists really deserve to be honored for it. I'm in a good position to confirm that, without certain journalists, we would never have been able to get a single idea across, particularly before October 1988. Tahar Djaout of *Algérie-Actualités*, Malika Boussouf, who does the program "Show Débat" on the radio channel 3, and others allowed us, quite simply, to exist. They took clear risks, and thanks to them, some breaches opened up in the system. We were able to steal a little of that confiscated air time. Second, journalists, along with the M.J.A.*, were the first to denounce the practice of torture in October 1988. Finally, throughout the period of 1989 to 1991 that we're discussing, the press became relatively free and played a central role. Without journalists, who covered the fundamentalists' acts of violence with great precision, we would never had known so much about what was happening. That's because the journalists who were government flunkeys continued to keep silent about such matters on the radio and television, whereas those who really did their job in those media despite the pressures they were under were constantly faced with the threat of being taken off the airwaves.

E.S.: What about singers?

K.M.: Well, on that subject, I must say that singers were, perhaps, the most important figures of the democratic ferment and of the resistance movement that followed it. They were the most efficient and popular opponents of both the F.L.N. and the F.I.S. You know, I have childhood memories that speak volumes about this. I remember that, to listen to the forty-fives of the old *raï*** singers, we would carefully close the windows because they had been banned from the airwaves by the F.L.N. These artists were never, never heard on the radio or television. They sang about love, about people's lives, just as they were, and they did it in the language of Algerians; that was enough to earn them the reputation of public enemies in the government's eyes. Little by little, Algerian *chaabi*** and Andalusian music would, the authorities believed, have to fade away in the face of Middle Eastern music. That's undoubtedly because these musical traditions showed the richness and the complexity of cultures in Algeria, whereas the party wanted to make everything uniform, the better to impose the Arabo-Muslim identity it promoted. I am reminded particularly of Chikha Rimiti, a marvelous woman who was the queen of raï: she was invited to sing at private parties, and men would pay great sums of money to hear her. A generation of artists died of asphyxiation during the thirty years when the F.L.N. was in power, because they didn't have access to any means of communication. And then, in the middle of the 1980s, raï exploded. Raï is Algerian, a type of music that exists neither in Morocco nor in Tunisia. It was destined to carry everything along in its wake, because the young raï singers who were starting out then, like Cheb Khaled and Raïna Raï, sang about their love life, their frustrations, their sexuality, their jobs, and their hopes, in their language and through an extremely sensual and stirring form of music; in the process, they rallied all the young people, thereby undermining the F.L.N. and the "Barbus." Raï, which was born in Oranie, soon transcended all regions and differences; it loosened people up, it encouraged them to talk about themselves, and to do it happily! When you're listening to raï, you're not Berber, or Chaouï*, or Tlemcenian, or French-speaking, or Arabic-speaking: you just are. You're an Algerian whom the government disdains and who says "fuck you" to that government, simply because you're listening to this music, which is apolitical but still a form of protest. Raï did play its part in the October 1988 uprising, because its singers had access to the radio before that date, thanks to a team of young disc jockeys whose program "Sans pitié" was the most popular throughout Algeria. Aziz Smati, Mohamed Ali Allalou, Sid Ahmed Semiène, Riad Kadour ... they opened the doors to freedom.

And then there is the very particular case of Kabyle singing, which has always gotten "special treatment" from the government. Aït Menguelet and Ferhat were incarcerated for their songs well before 1988; Idir left Algeria and, thanks to him, the new Kabyle music became known well beyond the country's borders; and, to mention just one more artist among many others, Matoub Lounès has always been a soldier of protest. Lounès is more than a symbol, he's a social phenomenon. He's a man whom both the government and the fundamentalists hold in contempt. Do you know that this very talented singer has never appeared once in his entire career on Algerian television? When Khaled became successful in France, the government consented to having his recordings played occasionally on the radio. Matoub has gotten nothing. It's true that he doesn't limit his songs to love and everyday life. He's a militant in the Berber Cultural Movement, a committed political activist, a spokesman, and a symbolic figure, and not just for the Kabyles. This popularity poses a real danger for everyone who is against democracy.

In short, from 1989 to 1991 all these musicians were met with enthusiasm by one camp and with fear by the other. The F.I.S. hated them all—it would, unfortunately, later become clear just how far the F.I.S. was capable of going, when Cheb Hasni [another raï singer] was assassinated in Oran and Lounès was kidnapped. These singers expressed a popular Algerian culture that the Islamists wanted to eradicate; they celebrated liberty, which was incompatible with religious fanaticism; and they unleashed the people's libido, which was diabolical for the fundamentalists, those killjoys. At the time, the F.I.S. members who controlled the A.P.C. "settled," if I can put it that way, for intimidating these singers by threatening them through their militias, in order to convince them to cancel their concerts and galas. Of course, the government was only too happy to allow this to go on. The raï festival in Oran was therefore banned by the Islamists.

E.S.: So did you equate the attitude of the government toward these singers with that of the F.I.S.?

K.M.: No, and I still don't today. The difference between the F.L.N. and the F.I.S. is that the former fights these singers because of what they sing about, whereas the latter does it because of who they are. The F.L.N. bans singers, whereas the F.I.S. kills them.

E.S.: Far away from Algeria, in January 1991, the Persian Gulf war broke out. It had well-known repercussions throughout the Arab world. In the name of your association, you sided wholeheartedly with Iraq. Why?

K.M.: This war was a heartbreaking affair, which involved nothing more than big money, oil, and the economic interests of the West, all disguised as a question of international law. Had anyone ever heard those same Western leaders protest, in the name of that law, the executions of Iraqi communists and democrats? Come on! I am viscerally revolted by injustice, and I cannot abide the idea that civilians, who are already repressed by an infamously violent dictator, should, all by themselves, face a coalition of thirty-five countries and pay with their lives for the strategic ambitions of the United States. In my view, Saddam Hussein cannot be confused with the Iraqi people, or vice versa. Now, as far as I know, Saddam is still alive, but some of the Iraqi people have perished.

What's more, I did not wait for the Gulf war to denounce the situation of women in Iraq. However, I think I've already said, rather heatedly, that no one could ever ask me to come to terms, even slightly, with the practices of Saudi Arabia, which is the clearest existing model of a fundamentalist state and which subsidizes all the Islamist movements on the planet. The Saudi women who defied the ban against women driving cars were, during this dirty war, arrested, imprisoned, and mistreated right under the noses of G.I.s who included American women in their ranks! Which nations who call themselves defenders of universal rights were moved by the plight of these women? Which ones intervened to defend them and demand that the Saudi monarchy adhere to international law? How, at the end of the twentieth century, can the U.S. and European governments support the most slave-loving country? Later, at the end of 1993, we held a meeting of women of the Maghreb in Tunis, and we declared: "We must overturn the Saudi monarchy!" If the United States really wanted to see democracy take hold in Muslim countries, all it would have to do is impose it where the money is: in the states of the Gulf region, which is the focal point of Islamism and a financial powerhouse. We've had quite a rough time of it, thanks to all those regimes! We'd like a little more justice, liberty, and democracy. But there was no question of that during the war. The Western governments chose their side: the side of a region that is utterly shameful from the perspective of human rights. So how could we trust them?

E.S.: So, given that you supported Iraq, did you accept the fact that Iraqi scuds fell on Tel Aviv?

K.M.: How could I accept that? I said that I was resolutely opposed to Saddam. The American authorities were completely responsible for those scuds. They knew perfectly well when they started the conflict that this madman would not hesitate to fire his missiles on Israel.

E.S.: How did you react to the position the F.I.S. took on the Gulf war?

K.M.: You know, during the first two weeks of the war, the F.I.S. was against Iraq and Saddam Hussein. In other words, it was on the side of its financial backer: Saudi Arabia. It held Saddam up to public obloquy and called him "Saddam el haddam," which means "Saddam the destroyer." But the base of the F.I.S., like all Algerians, could not accept seeing so many nations join forces against the only Arab country that had been a true friend during the Algerian war of liberation. To avoid isolating themselves from their base, the leaders of the F.I.S. turned their coats, quite tranquilly, after two weeks. In doing so, obviously, they went overboard. Ali Benhadj* appeared in a military uniform—which is forbidden by Algerian law—at the head of a demonstration outside the Ministry of Defense, to demand training camps and weapons so that Algerians could go out and fight alongside the Iraqis, his "brothers in Islam," as he called them from then on.

E.S.: And what were the consequences of these about-faces?

K.M.: Right after the Gulf war, because of the position of the Islamist parties in the various Muslim countries, a second fundamentalist International was created. It was led by Iran and Sudan and held its first convention in Khartoum. There, under the influence of Iran, new strategies for winning power were chosen; these were combined with intensified methods, like establishing training camps in the Sudan for the militants of the F.I.S.

Chapter 10
At the Heart of the F.I.S., Sexuality

Elisabeth Schemla: Even if you didn't imagine for a single moment that the F.I.S.* could prevail a second time in the legislative elections that were held in December 1991, you were obviously trying to figure out why this group fascinated the Algerian people. Was economic hardship an adequate explanation?

Khalida Messaoudi: It played an enormous part, of course. But that doesn't convince me altogether. Economic hardship was not the root of the problem, it simply fed it. I was listening to what the imams were preaching five times a day and to what the F.I.S. militants were proclaiming. I truly read everything they wrote, and I paid attention to the kinds of people who were the targets of their barbarous violence: it was there, necessarily, that the real explanation lay. And at the heart of their way of life, their mindset, their imprecations, and their savagery, I perceived a constant obsession, of the kind that is symptomatic of madness: an obsession with women. The truth is, no other theme looms as large as this one does in the ideology of the F.I.S. Without abusing a comparison that some might find overused or facile, the F.I.S.'s obsession with women is exactly like the obsession with Jews evident in the rhetoric of Hitler. According to the fundamentalists, women are the root of all evil. Or, rather, the salvation of the *oumma** lies in women's submission to the wishes of the imams. It is, moreover, no coincidence that feminists, who symbolize the women they abhor, are systematically called "Jew girls" by the Islamists; I'm one of the first to be referred to in this way, having been nicknamed "Barbra Streisand" by one of them.

E.S.: They always justify their obsession with women by referring to the sacred texts. Does Islam authorize that kind of interpretation?

K.M.: The fundamentalists invoke Islam to justify a priori and legitimize all their words and deeds. But I don't think any religious text, whatever it may be, contains within itself any orders about how it should be interpreted. It is what men make of it, depending on their political or social ambitions, and on their psychological makeup. There is, furthermore, a line in the Koran that reminds believers that all readings are possible but none is authoritative. Only God holds the truth of the message.

When I read *Colomba* by Prosper Mérimée, it reminds me of the status of women in traditional Algerian society. Yet, Colomba is Christian, and we are Muslims. One should not look for the answers in religion as a faith. Besides, Algerians have been Muslims for fourteen centuries, but emotional and sexual destitution has become an alarming social phenomenon only in recent years.

E.S.: If Islam is only a pretext, as you suggest, then what underlies this fixation?

K.M.: Sexuality. The fundamentalists, like any totalitarian movement, want to exercise absolute control over society, and they fully realized that the place to start was by seizing control of women's sexuality, something Mediterranean-style patriarchy facilitates. In addition, like all purifiers, they hate and persecute difference, which inevitably accompanies democracy. Now, what women represent is desire, seduction, mystery, trouble, and also alterity, which is immediately visible on their bodies. That is why the Islamists are so anxious to hide the female body, to veil it, to make biological difference disappear from the body's external signs. The women who refuse to submit to this become perfect targets, because they embody the Other that the fundamentalists need to mobilize and rally people to their cause. This was even easier in Algeria during the time when the fundamentalists were gaining influence, because women were the most vulnerable members of society and had been made even more vulnerable by the preexisting systems, colonization and then the F.L.N.*

E.S.: Yet for fundamentalism to take hold, there must have been a deep sexual and emotional frustration running through the population ...

K.M.: But that's exactly the case! Particularly among young Algerians. Sexuality is taboo in our societies, but you don't have to listen to speeches to know that this frustration exists, and that it is deep. The traditional social structures had been destroyed by colonization, and then families had been broken up by urbanization and industrialization. The clan had been pulverized. The balance that women and men had managed to find, at least within the clan, disappeared. In exchange, did they get freedoms and opportunities that would allow them to open up? No. But because the rules on separating the sexes which regulate personal life—and all the rules I described at the outset of this interview—have remained in place, many Algerians live today in total ignorance of the opposite sex. Obviously, the housing crisis I mentioned earlier only made the situation worse. This sexual distress had dramatic consequences. All that produced a very disturbed society, and the F.I.S. took advantage of it.

E.S.: Wasn't that sexual distress also grounded in the fact that relations between Algerian men and women have traditionally been very difficult?

K.M.: It is unquestionable that Mediterranean-style patriarchy taken to its extreme doesn't favor easy relations between the sexes, and that they always have an undercurrent of violence. In our culture, despite appearances, men are no more free to be themselves than are women. I am always struck by how difficult it is for our men simply to say "I love you." Even the most liberated men seem to find it truly painful to talk about tenderness and love. Their mothers play a major role in this problem, because they instill in their sons the vision of themselves they will have in the future. And that begins very early, beginning with circumcision. In our culture, circumcision is rarely practiced during the first few months after birth; it is usually done at the age of five or six years. Then it takes the form of a rite of initiation into virility. That's traumatizing, in my opinion. From that moment on, the immense threat that looms over boys who don't act "like men" is to be compared to girls. Mothers constantly tell them: "You're crying like a woman." Now, a woman is the most discredited being there is. After that, boys begin their schooling, which is a veritable training course in toughness. But when you get down to it, isn't that also true of many other societies, even today? Mothers not only steal their sons' childhoods, they inhibit them from living. And they act that way because their own status is at stake. They serve as the agents of men in dealing with boys just as they do with girls. For them, it's inextricable. Having said that, I'm well aware that this assessment is a bit hasty. You've asked a fundamental question that deserves a more competent analysis.

E.S.: Nonetheless, this situation is at the root of all the sexual abuse that a few courageous women have dared to discuss in public ...

K.M.: Of course, but this isn't the only type of sexual abuse. Male homosexuality, which is absolutely taboo, is another kind, because it isn't a choice that is made freely, in most cases. It is a practice to which men resort when there's nothing else available, and it can even take the form of raping young boys. We must also acknowledge all the abuse that is committed against children.

E.S.: In the privacy of the *hammam**, do women talk about that?

K.M.: And how! In the hammam, women tell each other everything; it's a place of fabulous complicity, where women warn each other about the sorts of things that go on within their self-enclosed houses. By a tacit agreement, all secrets are safe, and no one has to worry about any indiscretions. I love to listen to them, especially the matrons whom I call *les reliefs de l'Algérie* [in the sense of "the ones who still stand out"]. They're extraordinarily free in the way they talk. With them, too, it is extremely rare to hear them speak fondly about their husbands. What's more, such a woman never speaks of her husband by name—she calls him "He." As they bathe, these women complain about the beatings they've received, they slam their mother-in-law, of course, in an effort to kill her symbolically, and they exchange every possible and imaginable trick for "holding on" to the son, their husband. They criticize the second wife, polygamy being an endless subject for condemnation. Even though polygamy isn't widely practiced, they're haunted by it, and they're right to be. They attack the "asshole" who does that for sex and to have a second wife who can act as a supplementary work force. Sometimes they cry, and sometimes they laugh over their misfortunes, against which they rebel only in this private setting. There's no better place than this, during these long hours that provide women with the only comfort in their lives, for getting a real sense of the silent martyrdom they suffer on the outside ... But I was going to speak about this in the past tense, because the G.I.A.*, the Armed Islamic Group, has forbidden us from frequenting such bathhouses. Some women nonetheless continue to do so, despite the terror. Isn't that a marvelous act of resistance?

E.S.: Why was this ban imposed, given that women are there by themselves?

K.M.: I'll tell you an anecdote ... One day, at one of the public bathhouses, a girl in a *hidjab**, who was an F.I.S. militant, showed up in the changing room. She declared: "What you're doing is a sin, you're baring your bodies, and God doesn't like that." A woman who was a mother replied angrily: "You, you're going to teach me Islam? And tell me that I'm a nonbeliever? If you keep it up, I'll plunge you and your hidjab in the boiling water! You're the ones who are evil! That's all you think about!" She was right. And do you know why, according to these visionaries, it is dangerous for women to appear nude in front of each other? Because they might describe the body of another woman to their husband, and the husband could in turn go and repeat it to another man, and all that would bring discord, transmitted by a woman, the daughter of Satan!

E.S.: You've said that the F.I.S. took advantage of this state of affairs. That's undoubtedly because it offered an alternative. Now, what would that alternative be for women, judging merely from the comments that Madani* and Benhadj* have made on the subject? Would it consist in preventing women from working, turning them into "producers of Muslims," and other projects of this sort?

K.M.: Those projects prove that the F.I.S. has in no way liberated women: it has released them from their old shackles only to impose its own upon them. At the same time, we have to accept the obvious: the fundamentalists have seduced and even fascinated certain women. Why? Because it offers them a means of identification and self-affirmation that they no longer have, after all the upheavals I've described. It offers them something that traditional society, only traces of which still subsist, no longer provides. But it hasn't done this on the basis of Algerian tradition, since that is something it must combat in order to take power. Rather, the F.I.S. has adapted to the new situation of women, but in a way that could not be called modern. We shouldn't confuse the notion of modernity, which has a very precise meaning, with the flexible and subtle political tactic the fundamentalists have adopted, and whose only goal—a hidden one—is to arrive at an Islamic state which is supposedly original and idealized, and which has never existed.

Let's look at what has happened. The hidjab is one of the instruments of identification the F.I.S. has given women, but it isn't the only one. The F.I.S. has also provided them with a mode of political speech the F.L.N. never gave them, and that, in its democratic form, is exceedingly difficult to overcome. I've always been struck by the very peculiar behavior of the women who join the fundamentalist movement: they speak, whereas before they had obstinately kept their mouths shut! Suddenly, they have a way of speaking, ideas they can defend and for which they are even willing to go out and demonstrate in the streets—on orders, of course, but that's not the essential point. Even better, the F.I.S. gives them a place in which they can use this political speech, a place that tradition has always barred them from entering, a place outside. That is the mosque. The point of allowing women into the mosque is undoubtedly to have them praise and reproduce the ideology of the imam and its corollary, the supremacy of all things masculine. But women also acquire an identity there that is very difficult to contest, because it is endowed with an unparalleled power: the force of the sacred. A father, a brother, a mother-in-law can be opposed to many choices a woman might want to make: to work, or to take up art, for example. But how could they dare take on the self-proclaimed keepers of the holy message? This creates a certain abdication on their part, out of fear or tacit complicity. And that abdication on the part of relatives reinforces in women's minds their new sense of belonging to a world that presents some advantages.

That's not all. In the mosques, the F.I.S. performs one of the functions of the former clan system: marriage. On the walls of certain mosques, there used to be photos posted of women who were interested in getting married. In those mosques, cheap pamphlets were distributed that covered sexual problems and the way to solve them. With the F.I.S., militants get married among themselves, on an ideological basis. What progress, what a privilege compared to the difficulties I've discussed! Especially given that men and women can now get married without the consent of their families and without having obtained housing: all they need is the blessing of the instructor imam. It is no longer necessary to have a dowry, either. Fundamentalist marriage dispenses with that, which is an enormous opportunity in a society with so many penniless and unemployed young people. What this gives people is, in a word, an instant and inexpensive social status—and a certain sexual equilibrium. What a godsend! Women obtain this through a relationship that is recognized by the "party of God," even if it isn't recognized by society as a whole ... Lastly, for those who fail to find a partner, the F.I.S. takes care of that lack by proposing a means of sublimation through the exaltation of purity. There turned out to be quite a number of young people who had looked upon their situation as an absolute and definitive tragedy, and who embraced this solution, using faith as their justification. It made things much easier to bear—at least on the surface. For their sexual frustration subsisted, and violence was its only release.

E.S.: Hence the rapes, mutilations, and the decapitations that came later. Does this also explain, in your view, the "temporary marriage" that was introduced in 1991?

K.M.: I believe, in fact, that the *zaouadj el moutaâ** is yet another consequence of sexual frustration. This practice consists in forcing women to "marry" for a few hours or days. It was forbidden among Sunnites by the prestigious caliph Omar, but it is practiced by the Shiites, especially in Iran, and was imported into Algeria by F.I.S. militants who had been to Teheran or who had taken part in the Afghan conflict. But it's not very widespread, even in the F.I.S. This is nothing less than a disguised form of prostitution which these men have tried to impose, using God as an alibi. I'm not at all interested in knowing whether some women come to accept it because they see it as a chance to have sexual relations with a man, even though they lose everything in the process. I've been horrified to observe that all the women who refuse such "marriages" are abominably raped and killed. Last November, the press published photos of the remains of two sisters, one fifteen and the other twenty, who had not wanted to submit to a "temporary marriage." Believe me, it was impossible to look at those photos without wanting to throw up ... Unfortunately, this example is just one of ... I don't know how many cases, because we've never succeeded in determining an exact figure for this. All the testimony we've managed to collect shows that the phenomenon is significant.

E.S.: The fundamentalists also indulge in sexual abuse of children ...

K.M.: But they do it in the name of God. Even before the December 1991 elections, scandals had broken out. The newspaper *Horizons* reported on an incident that had occurred in Blida, the fundamentalist stronghold. An imam, who was an F.I.S. preacher, had become attached to a fourteen-year-old kid and raped him while they were visiting Oran. Many other details were known. The problem was figuring out how to make them public. Then, at the last minute, the government allowed the now-penitent preacher to appear on television—the better to justify repression, of course. Personally, everything that smacks of incrimination makes me deeply uncomfortable. And I asked myself why, instead of giving this man a public forum, our leaders didn't give one to us, who were proposing a different kind of society. It's always the same problem ... But I'll get back to the question at hand. In 1994, the G.I.A. kidnapped two preachers to serve on its Islamic courts; ordinarily, it is the "emir" who hands down "justice" there, but when he is not available, they need an imam who has been designated to replace him. The first of the two kidnapped men belonged to the Hamas* movement, which the F.I.S. suspected of having contacts with the government. This preacher, who was a major leader of the Islamic *daâwa**, refused to legitimize the *fatwas** that implied that certain targets should be beaten and killed. He was found mutilated, decapitated, and cut into pieces. The second man agreed to do what they asked of him. But he succeeded in escaping and, being very psychologically disturbed by what he had done and seen, he made some confessions. He described his journey through the land of the dead, before all of Algeria. Most notably, he described all the rapes of children to which he had been forced to give his "blessing."

E.S.: The newsletter of your association, the A.I.T.D.F.*, kept a very precise account of everything that the F.I.S. was inflicting on Algerians. You were ready—this time with your eyes fully open—to square off against Abassi Madani, the leader of the F.I.S., in a televised debate, where you'd been invited as one of the representatives of civil society. How did that debate go?

K.M.: The situation was extremely tense, because no one was happy with the electoral law. Women were being more and more openly targeted by the F.I.S. So were artists, already. Madani had attacked, among others, feminists like me, calling us "neocolonial-ist hawks" and "daughters of Joan of Arc" the day after a demon-stration we'd held on intolerance. In this show, "Face à la Presse," I spoke to him in Algerian Arabic, to be quite certain that all the viewers would understand me. First, I asked him to confirm what he had said. He did so, telling me that he had insulted us because we were against the Family Code*, which he declared was the only text that conformed to *charia**. Then I asked him about polygamy. He claimed that it was a duty under charia: "You're either for charia or you're against it." I raised the question of whether women have a right to be legally recognized as adults. He an-swered me, literally: "For us, women are adults when they reach puberty!" I really thought that his incompetence would astonish and disgust everyone. That wasn't the case. Then I got to the sub-ject of the program that encouraged women to go back to home and hearth, in return for subsidies that were "indexed according to their abilities." Where was Madani going to find this money, given that Algeria's coffers were empty? This was his reply: "We will do away with the police and the gendarmerie, and we'll apply that budget to these subsidies." Obviously, the job of policing morality in an Islamic state has to be done through militantism. In a word, he showed his true doctrinaire colors.

E.S.: Did you see him that night as a possible winner in the leg-islative elections, as someone who would become one of Algeria's central figures?

K.M.: No. For me, a man who confuses legal adulthood with pu-berty cannot claim to lead a modern state.

Chapter 11
The Interruption of the Electoral Process: Historic Error or Patriotic Duty?

Elisabeth Schemla: Why were the legislative elections that were supposed to be held in June, 1991 postponed?

Khalida Messaoudi: The F.I.S.* didn't like the mode of majority election with two rounds of voting which the government had adopted, or the division into made-to-measure constituencies, which greatly penalized everyone other than the F.L.N.* ... To my knowledge, it was French socialists who advised the Algerian government in this matter, which ended up costing us so much. By suggesting that Algeria use the same electoral procedures as are followed in France, they helped to nip in the bud the emerging democratic parties; for, in the Algerian context, only a system of proportional representation would have made real pluralism possible, and we feminists were perfectly aware of that. It seemed to me that these socialists did not protest, either, when they saw that women's right to vote was, in a sense, going to be "stolen" by their husbands in these elections. Fighting that would turn out to be a constant battle for feminists.

Having said that, I'll get back to the F.I.S. It decided to take power through the streets, as had been done in Teheran. It called for a paralyzing strike that was supposed to "shut down" the country, but the strike was a failure. Then it resorted to a "strike of civil disobedience" that was attended by barely six thousand F.I.S. members, who split into two groups demonstrating in two big public squares in the capital, Algiers. One of their slogans showed their real colors very clearly: "We don't want a charter or a constitution, we want to govern according to the Koran and the *hadiths**."

E.S.: The police and the Islamists had a violent confrontation. A state of siege was instituted, and the two leaders of the F.I.S., Madani* and Benhadj*, were jailed. They were sentenced to twelve years in prison. But the F.I.S. was not banned ...

K.M.: And that was not normal. But should we be surprised? Let's not forget that, at the end of a press conference held the day after the municipal elections of 1990, Madani had declared in front of all the Algerian and international journalists: "Chadli* is a great man!" And Chadli, in fact, refused to ban the F.I.S. This was all the more indefensible given that, at the time, all the Front's written and oral propaganda was violently attacking democracy; all you have to do is read their propaganda to see that. Every day, all over the country, the F.I.S. was denouncing democracy as a Satanic invention of Jews and the former colonial power, as an anti-nationalist, anti-Arab, and thus anti-Muslim model, and—to quote Ali Benhadj—as "impious" on top of that. They described it as the mother of monstrous secularism, which they compared to atheism. From 1989 on, Benhadj incessantly repeated that "there was no place for secularists, Berberists, communists, and so on in an Islamic society." There could be no doubt about the F.I.S.'s attitude and intentions. But no one took action—undoubtedly because no one thought the F.I.S. would prevail, because its disastrous management of the A.P.C.* had opened Algerians' eyes.

E.S.: The F.A.F.* [Brotherhood of Algerians in France], an organization that is closely tied to the F.I.S., claims that you were a candidate in the legislative elections and that you only got eight votes. What's that all about?

K.M.: That's obviously one of the many slanders the fundamentalists are so fond of. I did, in fact, appear on the ballot as an independent and feminist candidate in the elections that were supposed to take place in June. It was a fake candidacy, which I undertook to alert the public about the electoral law and the practices of the F.I.S. and F.L.N. I withdrew after making a public declaration in the newspapers and on television, before I'd even learned that these elections were going to be canceled. The eight votes, therefore, never existed, and I wasn't a candidate in December 1991 because women had reclaimed their right to vote.

E.S.: Why did the feminists win the case on the vote?

K.M.: We applied a great deal of pressure. Neither the government nor the courts were inclined to be equitable. No political party stepped in to say: "If women are not considered as full-fledged voters, we won't participate." But, once again, the *moud-jahidats** brought all their weight to bear by organizing a sit-in in front of the building that housed the head of the government. Their rallying cry was "One woman, one vote!"—which was a version of the slogan we'd adopted after the municipal elections: "Voting, like prayer, is something no one can do in your stead." We won with barely a month to go before the elections. So we didn't have nearly enough time to organize ourselves and run an effective campaign.

E.S.: During this time, the violence of the F.I.S. continued ...

K.M.: Obviously! But even so, the attack by an F.I.S. commando on the Guémar barracks in southwest Algeria, which occurred in November [1991], was a terrible shock. It was horrible. Eighteen recruits were found atrociously mutilated, with their sex organs cut off and stuffed in their mouths. For the first time, General Nezzar, the Minister of Defense, directly implicated the F.I.S. We were a few weeks away from an election that was still being presented, and experienced, as democratic and pluralistic.

E.S.: In the first round of voting, the fundamentalists won a majority even though they lost 1,200,000 votes. They'd achieved the ultimate victory. Where did you vote? Did you notice any irregularities during the voting?

K.M.: I voted in my neighborhood in El-Biar, and I myself didn't observe any anomalies. There was a good reason for that: the militant feminists of my association were in the polling stations and didn't let up for a minute in their vigilance. But elsewhere! Dead people and absentees voted. Women were forced by their husbands or brothers to use one ballot or another. A million voter identification cards from the F.F.S.* or the R.C.D.* never reached their destinations: that was because the F.I.S. held the majority in the city halls and was in charge of the electoral rolls. As soon as the polls were closed, I rushed over to the press room of the Ministry of the Interior to find out the initial results ...

E.S.: And?

K.M.: I'll always remember it ... At first, I had the feeling that the sky was falling. I was crushed, but I didn't sink into despair—not at all! It was immediately obvious to me: "Never, never, never this!" I had a choice: I could either go along with things and subscribe to formal democracy, which I knew would lead me to the slaughter-house; or I could refuse to do that because I didn't want to have an Islamic state for myself, or for women, or for my country. As I considered the second option, standing there in that ministry, I felt that I'd be acting in self-defense. And the women of Algeria would be, too ... Let's look at the figures:

number of eligible voters: 13,258,554
number of actual voters: 7,822,665
number of abstentions: 5,435,929
votes cast: 6,897,719
blank ballots: 924,906

In both rounds of voting, which were marked by a split between the F.L.N. and the F.I.S., the F.I.S. won a majority, gaining 3,260,222 votes—42 percent of the votes cast and 25 percent of all eligible voters. In other words, we were supposed to give Algeria to the F.I.S. so that it could transform the country into a killing ground, and do it for barely a quarter of the voters! That was out of the question! The only safeguard the Constitution provided was President Chadli, who'd been an open ally of the F.I.S. before the election. Let's go on with these numbers, because they provide another interesting insight. If you add up the abstentions and the blank ballots, there is a majority party that gained nearly six and a half million votes: this was the party that refused to choose between the F.L.N. and the F.I.S., which categorically rejected the confrontation that had been scripted.

E.S.: Do you mean to say that you suddenly thought about the possibility of interrupting the electoral process—something no one had at all envisioned, because no one believed the F.I.S. would win?

K.M.: Absolutely. And in the days that followed, I discovered that many, many people had spontaneously thought of the same possibility. I believe that people observing Algeria from outside the country did not truly understand exactly what these results signified for us. I refuse to allow anyone to judge us before taking into account, sincerely and honestly, this consideration: when one knows what a mortal danger a fascist party represents for a nation, does one have, yes or no, the right and the duty to put obstacles in its path, and to do it regardless of its audience? I grant that one could, provided one had the means, leave one's country, or form an intellectual circle and simply talk about principles in the abstract, without ever risking one's neck ... But that's not my style, or my choice.

E.S.: Weren't you at least concerned about the considerable frustration that would be felt by the millions of voters who, for the first time, had taken part in a vote that was a bit less rigged than usual?

K.M.: I accepted that consequence right away. There are moments in history when you have to be able to take full responsibility for the results of your actions. The resistance is not completely rosy. But it is the opposite of the utter darkness promised by Islamism.

E.S.: So what exactly happened?

K.M.: First of all, I got in touch with all the women in the associations that were akin to ours. On another front, we telephoned all our friends who belonged to the other big associations. One of my friends—Hafidh Senhadri, who was one of the first to be assassinated after 1992—informed me that people were talking about forming a Committee to Rescue Algeria that would include the women's associations, the National Union of public entrepreneurs, the organization of private entrepreneurs, the National Association of Public Administration employees, and probably the all-powerful General Union of Algerian Workers, with its three million union members. And that wasn't counting all the members of the liberal professions, the R.C.D. militants, and those of the Berber Cultural Movement. In other words, this committee would include virtually all the millions of Algerians who made up civil society—the leaders of the nation, who kept the country running. The next day, we in the A.I.T.D.F.* prepared a text and asked to meet with the Prime Minister, Sid Ahmed Ghozali. He met with us, and listened as we fearlessly reminded him of this Algerian proverb: "What you have done with your hands, you will undo with your teeth." He announced soon thereafter that the first round of voting had been validated, and that the second would be held as scheduled.

E.S.: Between the two rounds, the situation was truly dramatic. The term "crisis" is inadequate to describe what happened ...

K.M.: The electoral campaign resumed on the television. The

positions of everyone involved were clearly defined. On the F.I.S. side, an elderly spokesman named Mohamed Saïd, who had been in the Nazi S.S., presented the Front's program and asserted that neither renegade Muslims nor foreigners would be welcome in Algeria. Rabah Khébir, who was an F.I.S. leader and is now their representative in Bonn, said on television on January 2, 1992: "Anyone who doesn't vote for 'our' Islam will have to leave the country." During a conference with the international press, other party leaders warned: "Algerians will have to change the way they eat and dress." A word to the wise is enough! They added: "The Islamic state will be inspired by the Iranian, Saudi, and Sudanese models." Those aren't exactly democratic paradises. Finally, the new F.I.S. spokesman in Algeria declared, in referring to professional people who refused Islamism: "Personally, if I were them, I'd ship out. And we'll bring in shiploads of Muslim professionals." One last point: the lists of people who were to be evicted and executed had been drawn up and sent to the militants who'd been entrusted with carrying out the task. That's how I came to be warned about the danger I was in by a young member of the F.I.S., a Kabyle*, whose regionalist sympathies won out over his partisan duty.

E.S.: The R.C.D., which you supported, hardly won 230,000 votes. Can't this failure be seen as one of the principal reasons for its opposition to the continuation of the elections?

K.M.: For a new party, made up of young people, that result wasn't so bad, in my opinion. But it wouldn't have made any difference whether the R.C.D. had gotten five hundred thousand or a million votes. As soon as there was no longer any hope of counterbalancing the newly elected F.I.S. deputies in the Assembly, the R.C.D. had no choice. Saïd Sadi* made his decision after carefully studying the ballots. They were almost all favorable to the fundamentalists, who would have won by 80 percent. That result would have legally given them the possibility of rewriting the Constitution and applying *charia** in its entirety. The only shield against this modification of the Constitution would have been Chadli!

E.S.: Aït Ahmed*, for his part, wasn't at all in favor of interrupting the electoral process. It would deprive him of the legitimate recognition he'd been seeking for thirty years: the good results he'd gotten on the first round of voting, which augured well for the second round. He organized a demonstration in Algiers, which took place on January 2 and attracted three hundred thousand people.

K.M.: As far as Aït Ahmed's electoral success is concerned, the F.F.S. had 510,661 votes—in other words, 7 percent of the votes cast and only 4 percent of registered voters. That party got all the votes it could have gotten, and everyone knew it, including Aït Ahmed. The abstentionists of the Algiers region and Kabylia, who participated in that demonstration, came from districts that had already fallen into the hands of the F.I.S. or F.F.S. in the first round. The F.F.S. ran in thirteen districts, five of which also had the R.C.D. on the ballot. The F.F.S. could, therefore, have gone from twenty-five to thirty-eight seats at best. Under those conditions, I wonder by what miracle it could have countered the natural alliance of the F.I.S. and the F.L.N.

E.S.: Given that, wasn't Aït Ahmed's hostility toward the R.C.D. predictable? And wasn't his participation in the Rome meeting*, much later, also predictable?

K.M.: Aït Ahmed's opposition to the R.C.D. dates back to that party's creation. I believe he never accepted having a part of his own troops dissociate themselves from him in 1982 and go on to form another organization. He couldn't bear it, just like a father who refused to recognize the autonomy of his son. His fixation on the R.C.D. and the type of things he said about it, which were purely defamatory, proved that he was incapable of dealing with this party politically. I regret that Aït Ahmed did not understand that the R.C.D. and civil society had not called for stopping the elections to deprive the F.F.S. of what it was electorally "due"— what nonsense!—but rather because the elections were leading to a theocratic dictatorship. As for the rapprochement that occurred between the F.F.S., the F.L.N., and the F.I.S., it began long before Rome, right after the first round of the 1991 elections. I am sincerely sorry that the F.F.S. lost its half million votes. But if Ahmed was hoping to be compensated for that by allying himself with the F.I.S. and extricating himself that way, that's his business. No one should, however, ask me to define my own position according to the blackmail to which Aït Ahmed resorted when he said: "It's either my votes or war against the R.C.D."

E.S.: When you wholeheartedly embraced the idea of interrupting the elections, didn't you realize that the F.I.S., once stripped of its victory, would step up its barbarism? Shouldn't you have anticipated and predicted the infernal cycle of violence and repression which would ensue?

K.M.: Your question presupposes that the violence of the F.I.S. was a response to the interruption of the elections. In truth, the facts are there to demonstrate that this violence went much farther back. I know that many observers, who were either really ignorant of the situation in Algeria or had ulterior motives, have tried to substantiate that theory. Frankly, I find the theory scandalous and even insulting for Algerians, who have had to face the actions of the F.I.S. for a long time. I have devoted myself to relating, as honestly as possible, I think, everything that has been going on for several years in my country. Nothing was confidential or secret. Any journalist, diplomat, or foreign executive can see, read, and witness. Moreover, if the violence of fundamentalism was just a reaction of rebellion against the interruption of the electoral process, how do you explain the violence of Egyptian or Bengalese fundamentalists, who sow death without any elections being held? I repeat that we are dealing with a brand of totalitarianism, and that violence is consubstantial with it.

E.S.: Under those conditions, why didn't anyone demand that the F.I.S. be banned and the elections canceled before they took place?

K.M.: That's undoubtedly the best question one could ask. I don't have a satisfying answer. The communists were the only ones to call for a boycott. Perhaps we were stuck, in spite of ourselves, in the dilemma we sometimes voiced among ourselves: "When you're a democrat, you can't be opposed to elections."

E.S.: Between the two rounds of voting, you were one of the first, if not the first, to demand that Chadli be deposed.

K.M.: That occurred in a meeting organized by the women's association of the Committee to Rescue Algeria on January 9, 1992. The Trotskyist women weren't there. I was in a state of intense emotion and intense determination. From the rostrum, I asked everyone to stop focusing on the F.I.S. And I said: "Chadli is the F.I.S.'s first short circuit, and he has officially declared that he would share power with the Islamists ... We have to blow him up! I speak in favor of stopping the elections! All they are, in fact, is a transfer of power, dressed up as a legal process, between the government and the fundamentalists!" I had absolutely no idea at that moment that, two days later, the electoral process would indeed be interrupted. I said what I said quite innocently, but without any ill humor. For me, quite simply, there was no other way.

E.S.: With the resolute support of civil society, the army—or rather, one clan of the army—forced Chadli to resign on January 11, 1992. The National Assembly was dissolved, and the elections canceled. It was a paradoxical coup d'état: a handful of generals, followed by a generation of young officers, turned one government upside down and blocked the emergence of another, in the name of democracy. Did you support it without reservation?

K.M.: The army clan that carried out this coup d'état was acting on its own behalf and for its own reasons. I didn't necessarily have the same reasons as it did for wanting to stop the damage these elections were doing. I would always be separated from all the men in the regime (plus several others ...) by the Family Code* and the situation of women. But our interests converged circumstantially. It just happened to be an army clan that was achieving what I had hoped for, and that had the means to do it. When I saw that not everyone in the military was a Chadliist, and that there were some officers who were, if I can allow myself this comparison, followers of De Gaulle and of his resistance to collaboration, I realized that our views were similar. In my eyes, interrupting these particular elections was a patriotic duty, and it's very difficult for me to grasp that some people might not understand that Algeria, in January 1992, was literally in danger of dying. I had absolutely no idea that, in a few days, Boudiaf* would be in charge of the country. I wouldn't even have been able to conceive of such a thing! He was far away, elderly, no one had seen him in Algeria for thirty years, and no one ever spoke of him. Who could have imagined—other than those who brought him back—that he would be the man of the hour? Really, no one could.

E.S.: The H.C.E.* [High State Committee] that the army put in place did in fact choose Mohamed Boudiaf as its leader. What were your initial reactions when you learned of this?

K.M.: They were divided. On the one hand, he was a legendary figure for whom I had great respect. He was one of the founders of independent Algeria, one of its historic leaders. You don't often find in our country an opposition leader, a socialist, who makes no compromises on his principles. Boudiaf had been arrested, tortured, and condemned under Ben Bella*. He had succeeded in escaping to Morocco, where he had settled and become the manager of a brickyard. On the other hand, I felt disappointed: "They've gone, yet again, and dug up an old guy from the F.L.N.; we'll never see the end of it!" And then, on January 16, he made his first live speech on the television. What a surprise! He was a tall, thin man with an emaciated face that was really quite unusual. And he spoke with his hands, just as we Algerians do. In a word, he had a distinctive appearance. And there was another surprise: he spoke in Algerian, in street Arabic! He even switched into French occasionally! Like everyone else, I couldn't believe my ears. It was the first time in my life that I had heard one of our heads of state, one of our politicians, abandon classical Arabic and address the people in their own language. Then came the shock. What did he say? "The mission of the F.L.N. ended in 1962. Come on, it's time the F.L.N. left for the history museum!" How can I describe it to you? It was a kind of infatuation, which never wore off for five and half months.

E.S.: It was an infatuation that many shared. The cartoonist Dilem invented a nickname that soon became popular in the streets, "Boudy." That's something that had never been seen in Algeria. What were Boudiaf's special traits?

K.M.: He could speak bluntly to Algerians. For example: "Algerians, it seems, are proud. But where is their pride when they allow a woman to be mistreated before their very eyes?" Things that people would never have accepted from anyone else, from him they took. He commanded respect because we understood that he wasn't like those who had dragged us to this point. We were a people that had been orphaned since the death of Messali Hadj* and that had finally found a father, whose authority we respected and for whom we felt affection. In a very short time, Boudiaf performed a miracle: he began to reconcile Algerians with themselves, with their history, with their image. He taught us how to believe in ourselves again, and to think that we hadn't been struck with any curse and that regression was not our destiny. Algerians began to love Algeria again.

E.S.: He adopted a hard policy toward the F.I.S. The Front was dissolved on March 4, 1992, the mosques were reclaimed, and the militants who'd been arrested were sent to camps in the South ...

K.M.: Boudiaf initially tried to dissociate the movement's young members from its leaders. He told them that there was no point in repressing someone who had gotten on the wrong track by taking up arms. What had to be changed were all the conditions that had led such a person to that extreme. "The F.I.S. militants are our children, and I'm holding out my hand to them ... I beg them to conduct their political struggle while respecting people's lives and property ..." But he did not let the leaders, big or small, off lightly. A few weeks later, he said unequivocally: "I will never negotiate with anyone who kills Algerians, or with his silent partners." That was a direct allusion to the F.L.N., a group with which Boudiaf never wanted to meet, because he was familiar with what it had done in the past and knew that it was filled with Islamists who were really working for the F.I.S. Once again, this was the first time a president had dared to say such things. For us, it was obvious that Boudiaf was going to try to reform the institutions and the system in the direction we wanted: by putting an end to the F.I.S. and the F.L.N. It was a breath of fresh air! At the same time, he decreed that justice should also be done in regard to the young militants who had been sent to the camps in the South because they were suspected of Islamism: about two weeks before his assassination, he freed six thousand of the eight thousand detainees.

E.S.: Boudiaf came back into contact with an Algeria he no longer knew. He consulted others a good deal, and took the pulse of the country. He met with you ...

K.M.: I went to see him, at his request, one afternoon at his residence. He wanted to chat with me as president of a feminist association. As you might suspect, the first subject that I—we—spoke about was women and the Family Code. I described the situation to him as precisely as possible. But, because I am also a teacher, he asked me many questions about the school system, about the damage that had been done by Arabization, and about the decline in the average level of students. I realized that this was going to be one of his pet subjects. He also told me that he intended to establish an organization that would be charged with devising projects for the High State Committee [H.C.E.]. He hoped that some young people active in civil society would be involved in it. This was a man who had decided to straddle the generations by reaching out to the generation that had no scores to settle with the past, that had not aligned itself with the F.L.N., that was keeping things going and trying to salvage certain values. Curiously, he asked me if the members of this organization should be paid, and I said no. I was struck by two things: Boudiaf was modern, or rather modernist, and he exuded integrity. We parted very cordially. I was thrilled with this man.

E.S.: The National Advisory Council [C.C.N.*] was established. You were one of its sixty members. Was this a stroke of luck for you?

K.M.: It was a unique opportunity. When one of Boudiaf's advisors called me to ask if I was interested in this position, I didn't hesitate for an instant! It was clear that Boudiaf's revolutionary spirit was unwavering. For me, for my generation, it was completely unexpected to be asked to participate in an organization that was supposed to contribute to putting Algeria on the path to democracy. At the C.C.N., I focused on women and education. We were in a strange political situation where a High State Committee held both presidential and legislative powers after a coup d'état, but very quickly seemed much more credible than if it had been generated by an electoral process. It was a miracle. The role of the C.C.N. was to elaborate proposals each time the H.C.E. asked it to. They might or might not be adopted; that was the rule of the game.

E.S.: What were the reforms Boudiaf wanted to undertake right away?

K.M.: He was obsessed with the school system, which he considered to be unworthy of the Algerian people. Since he wasn't a Kabyle, and thus couldn't be suspected of Berber sympathies, he reopened the question of Arabization, and repeated in all his speeches that the education system would have to be dismantled and entirely rethought, in terms both of content and of language of instruction. He wanted to be rid of the fundamentalist indoctrination that his predecessors had allowed into the schools. He knew how to reach young people by talking to them about culture, openness to the modern world, technical studies and the sciences, and high-quality diplomas. When he mentioned unemployment and promised jobs, no one laughed.

E.S.: Why?

K.M.: Because, shortly after assuming power, Boudiaf condemned and denounced the generalized corruption that had become a style of management for all the F.L.N. members who had been squandering money for years and years. He coined the term "politico-financial mafia" to describe those who had helped themselves to the country's money, using it to open personal accounts in Switzerland and elsewhere. Algerians were immediately receptive to this: nothing could have warmed their hearts more. He said openly what everyone was thinking, what everyone was enduring. "I know that this mafia is the source of your tragedy!" I remember that, when we heard this sentence for the first time, we said to ourselves: "Well, the first person who opposes the Algerian regime is the president himself!" Boudiaf was a daily event. We didn't know how right we were, unfortunately.

E.S.: Concretely, what did he do to fight corruption?

K.M.: He appointed hand-picked investigators and gave them full authority to poke around in the D15. The D15 is a decree that allows people to import and export merchandise. Because the D15 was often applied in a way that favored clients or was falsely authenticated by corrupt customs agents, money was misappropriated and all sorts of high-scale trafficking took place. Some scandals erupted, and certain networks were dismantled. So, of course, Boudiaf was sticking his nose into something that was too dangerous. The entire regime was implicated, and how many in the military were not involved? He was becoming bothersome, too bothersome. But we, who were so happy to see him doing all this, didn't realize just how much trouble he was causing.

E.S.: Was he also ready to tackle the Family Code, and thus take on all the supporters of charia?

K.M.: Yes. I never saw the president in person again, but I met Mrs. Boudiaf several times, and I found her to be a woman who worked actively on behalf of women. I think she knew how to show her husband that he had to put an end to all that. I learned, in fact, that he reproached his advisors for failing to tell him about the Code, "a very big problem," and said that they should immediately create a commission whose job would be to study how to abolish it. In the last speech he made, in Annaba, he spoke about women, and about the need to build a society in which they would be respected: "A society without women is a loathsome society."

E.S.: Boudiaf stepped on a lot of toes, challenged too many interests, and became irksome. His weakness was that he was acting alone: he wasn't a member of the seraglio, and he had neither a clan nor a network to support him. Civil society and its representatives, with whom he surrounded himself, had no influence with those who really held power. Boudiaf was put in office by the army to save the face of a regime that was rotten to the core, but he erred by taking his mission seriously. In your opinion, what was it that led definitively to his condemnation?

K.M.: It was no secret that Boudiaf was preoccupied with the circumstances surrounding his nomination. He never stopped telling his entourage: "Even if I am popular, I am not legitimate, and I refuse to stay in this situation. If I want to have free rein, I must be elected by the people, if the people decide things that way ..." He thus began thinking about and working on presidential elections, which he wanted to hold well before the dates that had been proposed when the H.C.E. was set up. He talked about holding them at the end of 1992, he designed a project for a national patriotic rally, he made contact with the democrats, and he proposed declaring his candidacy on the basis of a clear and short appeal to republican principles: the democratic rotation of offices, parliamentary pluralism, a state based on rights, justice, freedom of expression, and so on. He wanted to prepare for the transfer of power to the young generation: "We waged the war. Now we must let the young take their turn in working for the country!" We, for our part, were enthusiastic ... But we were far less quick than his assassins in realizing that his project would succeed, that he was going to be elected, and that it would change the face of Algeria. We only understood this on the day he was buried. When you're not oriented toward the culture of graft and intrigue, it is difficult to imagine that your country is about to indulge in the "luxury" of such a political assassination.

E.S.: On June 29, 1992, while on an official visit to Annaba, Boudiaf was shot in the back, in front of the television cameras, while giving a very powerful speech on "breaking with the past." It was a moment of horror and shock. No one believed the theory that he was killed by a "crackpot" with Islamist sympathies who shot him on impulse because he was waging war against the Islamists. What do you think?

K.M.: The assassins of Mohamed Boudiaf are still in power. President Zeroual* knows them quite well. Justice has never been served. As long as the truth hasn't been told, the crisis of confidence between the Algerians and their leaders will persist. Nothing constructive can be done until then. As long as the people responsible for Boudiaf's death are leading this country, resistance is, once again, the only answer. The alchemy that was produced between this man and the Algerians was a miracle. At his funeral, didn't we see young Islamists who were disconcerted by his message and wanted to wish him well? I haven't given up hope that this could happen again.

E.S.: Do you really think that Boudiaf managed to reach young people who had gotten involved in fundamentalism?

K.M.: Some of them, yes, and anyone can confirm that for you. Boudiaf's impact on Algeria's youth also affected the troops of the F.I.S., which was deeply shaken by it. Here's proof: Boudiaf was able to ban praying in the streets, and to have the motto of the Algerian state reestablished over the entrances to the town halls, without triggering the predicted bloodbath. It wasn't until after his death that the violence resumed.

E.S.: Since you accuse the government of assassinating Boudiaf, why did you stay on the C.C.N. until the very end of its mandate, in January 1994?

K.M.: That may have been a mistake on my part. But I talked it over with my friends and fellow militants. We thought that it was better for me to stay on the Advisory Council so that I could use it as a forum for denouncing the betrayal of the H.C.E. and the army in regard to Boudiaf. That's what I did, as my public statements from the time attest. Then, beginning in March 1993, the Islamists adopted their strategy of targeted violence against intellectuals. The first three victims, on March 16 and 17, were Djilali Liabes, a former Minister of Higher Education, and Hafidh Senhadri and Ladi Flici, who were both members of the C.C.N. along with me. I was about to be condemned to death myself. I couldn't even consider the idea of deserting the cause at that point.

E.S.: What was at stake, finally, with Boudiaf?

K.M.: The definition of an individual and collective identity. Claiming that there is a split between those who embrace an Arabo-Muslim identity and those who chose modernity, as some people have insisted, is tantamount to masking the complexity of

Algeria. Boudiaf, along with a certain number of pacifist democrats, wanted our country to forge an identity that wasn't for or against Arabia or the West, but rather near to both. This is the heart of the entire stakes, the entire struggle: will Algeria choose to enter into the modern age through democracy or through totalitarianism, which are the two contemporary models?

E.S.: When Boudiaf died, did you lose hope?

K.M.: I was deeply unhappy. I was also immensely proud to have been able to work with this man. And I know I will continue to fight, because he showed that it is possible to prevail.

Chapter 12
Is There a Way Out of the Impasse?

Elisabeth Schemla: Three years have gone by. Algeria has, in the meantime, sunk into an unprecedented state of general violence. Between thirty and forty thousand people have been killed, the victims either of fundamentalism or of the security forces; some of them were foreigners. For 1994 alone, it is estimated that 6,800 children, women, and men were assassinated by the terrorists, while the repression by the government also increased and was often inflicted without distinction on working-class neighborhoods that were Islamist strongholds. It wasn't until the first assassinations of intellectuals and journalists occurred—that is, until the armed groups of the F.I.S.* changed strategies—that international opinion became aware of the stakes. For you, what does this new strategy signify?

Khalida Messaoudi: The Islamists believe they have to clear the country of all the people who really bother them. They have to kill intelligence, creativity, the republican alternative, life. By targeting the elite, they are targeting Algerian society itself, because none of my friends who have been shot down, one after the other, had anything to do with the government. In their war, the Islamists make no mistakes. The targets they choose are people who defend the only project for society that is radically different from that of the Islamists, doing so not necessarily from within a political party but in their day-to-day commitment, in their way of carrying out their professional responsibilities. The goal of the fundamentalist strategy is to force the elite into exile or impotence. Thanks to the independent press, intellectuals nonetheless continue to express themselves and pursue their work. But the noose is tightening around the designated victims, and one of the tragedies we've had to bear is the indifference the government has shown toward this murdering of the mind. Because it is the government's potential or declared opponents that are being executed by the Islamists, they're doing it a favor. Moreover, it will take years for Algeria to find men and women of the quality and integrity of those who have died. That crime is unpardonable.

E.S.: Do you think that repression is a solution? You supported the National Committee Against Torture in 1988, and you obviously can't approve of repression now that it is directed against the Islamists ...

K.M.: Responding to terrorism with a kind of repression that falls essentially on the militants of the F.I.S., while sparing its leaders and silent partners, cannot be a solution. In essence, terrorism is unacceptable. We cannot simultaneously defend a democratic project and tolerate practices that are contrary to the very values for which we are now dying. However difficult it may be for them to uphold law and order, the security forces have to understand that they can accomplish that only through a strict application of the laws of the Republic. Here, again, the future of democracy is at stake. In short, I don't accept torture.

Unfortunately, torture is an integral part of this regime. My friends got a "taste" of that, too, on several occasions! Saïd Sadi* bears indelible marks of this brand of torture from the time he spent in the Lambèze penitentiary in 1986. Now, I have never seen any humanitarian organizations, or the French left, get overly worked up about this or mobilize about it, as they are now doing for the F.I.S. ... As long as I am alive, I will testify that neither Amnesty International nor any league for human rights has even come to ask for a copy of the death sentence that was issued against me. I had hoped that my case, and that of many of my friends, would interest them, at least as information. But I've heard nothing from them. I will not comment on their motivations; I'm simply stating a fact. It doesn't surprise me that the government of my country won't protect me, and I don't expect anything from it. On the other hand, for me to have to justify my opinions, my positions, and the meaning of my struggle—right down to the fact that I am still alive—before skeptics, that's repugnant. There's nothing innocent about this. Why is it that every time I try to speak about the tragedy that has befallen civil society and the democrats, people immediately counter by evoking the "martyrdom" of the fundamentalists, as if I were responsible for it? Furthermore, not all causes are equal, in my view: fundamentalism, like racism, is not an opinion, it's a crime.

E.S.: Keeping the army in power cannot, therefore, be a solution, in your opinion?

K.M.: Certainly not! The army has proven its absolute inability to govern. What's more, I don't see how it could maintain power indefinitely against all the rest of society. The clan of President Zeroual* is not opposed to the basic objectives of Madani*, but it is entertaining an impossible "dream": the dream of an Islamism without terrorism. That ignores the motives which have pushed a portion of Algeria's youth into the arms of the F.I.S. Algerian fundamentalism is an extremism that was borne not of conviction, but of despair and the desire for revenge. The army would have to be prepared to propose concrete answers to that despair, in order to put an end to the violence. That is not at all the case.

E.S.: What is the state of the ideological forces within the army? Are there, to your knowledge, republican officers with whom the democratic camp could work?

K.M.: The army is not a homogeneous bloc—that's no revelation. At least two large tendencies coexist in it, one favorable to Islamism, the other not. In this second camp, there are some people who really have republican convictions, and some who are opposed to the F.I.S. because it has given them no guarantees on the safety of their lives and properties. Are the republicans legion? I've heard that there are several young career officers, trained in the top schools, who are not implicated in the shady deals of their elders. Why don't they come and support us, if they exist? It's not up to us to go to them! But I don't know anything more about that ... Whatever the case may be, the army today is practicing a juggling act between these two tendencies that is perilous for Algeria. The facade of unity cannot hold up indefinitely. So basing our positions on the army as a deus ex machina, and defining our strategy according to it, would just reinforce its self-image as the decisive actor and inevitable arbiter. That would end up getting us even more entangled in the system that has been strangling us for thirty years. There is, in my view, no solution other than the autonomous construction of a democratic republican force—one strong enough to be the alternative that will save Algeria. That can only be conceived as entailing two breaks: a break with the regime, whose backbone is the army, and a break with its fundamentalist offspring. In other words, I am also resolutely opposed to the "enlightened military dictatorship" that certain people dream about.

E.S.: Would it still be possible for the F.I.S. to take power by itself?

K.M.: If it could do that, it wouldn't pass up the opportunity. But I think that the F.I.S. is far less able to take control of the streets than it was in 1991. Its relentlessness in attacking civilians shows that it is incapable of mobilizing them. It is militarily weakened by the security forces, politically slowed down, and morally discredited, because the assassinations of children and the rapes and decapitations of women have shocked to the utmost a society whose code of honor cannot tolerate such acts.

E.S.: Do the internal divisions within the F.I.S., and the fact that it has splintered into rival armed groups that are nearly autonomous and have no national coordination, even if they are in contact with the political leaders, play a role in this powerlessness?

K.M.: The Islamist movement is plagued by conflicting strategies over methods or targets, by the divergent ambitions of leaders who are pushing their troops into the insane logic of murderous excess, and by the contradictory interests of the countries that drive them. The "Afghan" F.I.S. militants in the service of the United States cannot get along with the groups that are controlled by Qaddafi. Those who are financed by Saudi Arabia cannot work alongside those who are maintained by Iran or Sudan. All of them reproduce on Algerian soil the quarrels, hatreds, and incompatibilities of their foreign allies. On top of that, Algerian Islamism is missing something that is not lacking in Egypt, nor in Iran, nor in Sudan: a politico-theological personnel that is native to those societies, and that is ready to organize the Islamic state. It's all those things that, in our country, make the Islamists incapable of taking power ... Many people believe we're dealing with a unified armed force that has a well-considered national strategy and is united under the banner of the Islamic Salvation Army [the armed branch of the F.I.S.]. The reality is quite different. We are faced with a multitude of self-created mini-groups, each one of which operates on its own account. Only the G.I.A.* is an exception. It is better organized because it has international contacts and is linked to all the other big terrorist networks that are coordinated by the Iranian secret services. For example, it recently met in Lebanon with the Lebanese Hezbollah, the Palestinian Islamic Djihad, and the Egyptian Islamic Djihad. But even the G.I.A. lacks the force of conviction and the means to accede to power all by itself.

E.S.: The democrats, for their part, are finding it difficult to attain a public existence, and they are terribly divided. Why?

K.M.: The government does everything it can to prevent a democratic front from forming. It has tried, first of all, to deny the democrats any space for free public expression. It has blackmailed the independent written press by abusing its monopoly on paper and the means of expression. It uses the security system as a pretext to silence the press, whenever it pleases. It even concocted a law that forbids enterprises from directly choosing their own advertising support: advertising is distributed in proportion to proofs of docility. Here's an example of the government's refinement of perversity: in March 1995, a Francophone publication was suspended because it hadn't yet produced an Arab-language equivalent! As for the so-called public service television and radio, the government always uses them as its private property. In other words, you have to pledge allegiance to win access to the microphone or screen. Saïd Sadi, for example, has not appeared on any political program in four years. As for me, I've not had the right to appear on Algerian television since the assassination of Boudiaf*. Fortunately, the French stations that can be picked up in Algeria occasionally give me a forum ... Since June 29, 1994, we've realized—and at a heavy price, with two people dead and seventy-one wounded, including myself—that autonomous political movements can rely only on themselves to ensure their safety. The government washes its hands of that. I should emphasize that we can hardly have any public meetings any more these days. Only the famous "spontaneous demonstrations" in support of Zeroual are allowed to take place. The threats from the fundamentalists, and the living conditions they force upon us, make it difficult for militants to meet, to exchange ideas, and to devise common strategies. Finally, it's true that unhealthy political mores prompt certain leaders, unfortunately, to sacrifice honest debate to their personal antipathies. That spoils the climate, aggravates dispersion, and disconcerts a people that can no longer find its bearings.

E.S.: Doesn't that make a democratic project a pure utopia?

K.M.: We have no other choice. Even if our engine has stalled, we'll have to figure out how to work together one of these days. The pressure of events and of a population that aspires to such a union will force us to. What's crucial today, in Algeria, is not to promote a program, but rather to bring about the triumph of sacred values like liberty, the respect for human dignity, justice, and equality. A country is at stake, not a party. It was in this the perspective that the Movement for the Republic, on which I serve as one of the vice presidents, was founded in November 1993. It is a group that was created by 5,112 citizens, acting outside of their political cliques, but to promote the establishment of a minimum level of democratic freedom.

E.S.: Wasn't the Rome platform*, which gathered together other political structures in January 1995, also an attempt to find a way out of the crisis?

K.M.: On that subject, we have to distinguish between form and substance. In Rome, we've been told, the democratic opposition met with the F.I.S. First, let's talk about that democratic opposition. Who was there? Principally, the F.L.N.* and the F.F.S.* How, through what miracle, could the former ruling party, the author of the Family Code*, which never repudiated any of its actions, have transformed itself? The fact that Abdelhamid Mehri, the F.L.N.'s secretary general, is opposed to Zeroual does not imply that he has any objective other than regaining power. That's the first fraud of the Rome meeting. As for the F.F.S., all it did was lend a tone of democratic authenticity to those agreements. As for the rest, the people gathered around the table were fundamentalist negotiators: Ben Bella* for the M.D.A.* [Movement for Democracy in Algeria]; Ali Yahya* and Anwar Haddam, an avowed member of the G.I.A., for the F.I.S.; and Abdallah Djaballah for En-Nahda.*

At bottom, the accords they reached were a bunch of contradictory declarations superimposed on each other. Everyone can find what he or she wants in them. The essential thing, in my view, is that on the non-negotiable principles, the signatories affirm the "superiority of legitimate law." In juridical terms, that means that *charia** is superior to civil laws. Here are two examples: divine law accepts polygamy, so the signatories of Rome are committed to never putting it into question; and divine law recommends cutting off the hand of thieves and killing apostates, so this can be done legally. It's easy to understand that I could never advocate such a future. Given the nature of these accords, how long can we continue to say that the F.F.S. is still democratic, since it accepts such monstrosities?

E.S.: Yet didn't the F.I.S., under certain conditions, commit itself to renouncing violence?

K.M.: If that wasn't the most tragic thing about the situation, it would be laughable! The F.I.S. made peace in Rome and continued the war in Algeria. A week after the San Egidio meeting, a car bomb went off at rush hour in the center of Algiers and caused a bloodbath. Who immediately claimed responsibility for the act? None other than Anwar Haddam, who signed the Rome accords in the name of the F.I.S., and who is also the F.I.S. spokesman in Washington. I'm not surprised that none of the other "Romans" saw fit to denounce him. But I am surprised that no one else was indignant about that silence, particularly in France. The negotiators stand by all the actions carried out by the terrorist groups. Although it may have been an astute media event, this platform is null and void.

E.S.: François Mitterand was one of its staunchest defenders. What do you think about his support?

K.M.: Mr. Mitterand was always mistaken about Algeria. During the war of liberation, when he was Minister of the Interior, he maintained that there was "only one solution, war." After independence, as First Secretary of the Socialist party, he turned a blind eye to the Boumediene* regime. Once he became President of the Republic, he persisted in his error by supporting Colonel Chadli* as president, and then he disapproved of the interruption of the electoral process. On the Rome question, he sent us his last poisoned present.

E.S.: How angry you seem! Do you feel the same way in regard to the entire French left?

K.M.: I'm not angry. As for the French left, it is not monolithic. At every stage in its historical development, the left has always contained certain people who were more lucid and faithful to its values. But I'd particularly like to address what's on my mind to certain leftist intellectuals. I can accept that they may have scores to settle with their own "Algerian history." But they should stop doing it at the expense of my generation! Some of them are old enough to be my father or mother. I cannot possibly share their problems and their resentments. I am not responsible for what bothers them, or for their disappointment over the fact that their dream for a socialist Algeria, an Algeria that would be "the beacon of the Third World," was not realized. The generation to which I belong is capable of thinking on its own, of choosing its own references—including its bibliographical references—and of dispensing with outside approval. I'm very pleased that intellectuals and researchers are fascinated with Islam as a subject of study. But they can't ask me to discover or embrace their vision of a religion, a culture, and a patrimony in which I myself was raised, in which I am steeped. I respect their status as observers, so they should do the same toward my status as a participant, which is totally different. Has anyone ever seen a chemist demand an explanation from a molecule he is analyzing? And why should Islam get special treatment?

E.S.: What do you expect from France?

K.M.: I know that France's policy toward Algeria is heavily influenced by our common history, as well as by immigration, natural gas, uranium, and the oil reserves that have just been found to be enormous. However, what strikes me about the current crop of French politicians is their range of opinions on my country: there are virtually as many different positions as there are officials. That is a sign that they are both aware of the stakes and reluctant to take a decision, which I understand. France has to manage bilateral relations that are becoming more and more complex, because a new player is stepping in and clouding the issue: the United States. America, whose geo-strategic and economic interests have long made it the ally of the Islamic states, would be perfectly content if the fundamentalists prevailed. France should not resort to cutting deals with the Islamists, as well, simply to outbid the United States and defend its own claim to leadership in Algeria. I'll take the liberty of reminding people that the Islamist leaders have already clearly chosen Washington. I do not, however, mean to imply that Paris should continue to support the Algerian regime. To the contrary, I am astonished that France, a republican and secular nation, is dragging its feet about accepting and supporting its natural allies: the democrats who are leading the resistance in Algeria and who refuse any alliance with "fascislamism." I implore France to listen to this: the handful of voices like mine, who have been lucky enough to get media attention, are not alone. In Algeria, they are the echo of a civil society that is waiting to be heard. In France itself, those voices express the declared choices of the immigrant community, as has just been proven by an exclusive poll conducted by *Valeurs actuelles* and Europe 1. The overwhelming majority of Algerians who have settled in France support the democratic republican project, reject fundamentalism, and practice Islam quite peacefully in a secular setting.

E.S.: Let me ask you a precise question with regard to Islam. Shouldn't the Algerian democrats use it as a reference point, to insure that their message is understood and advanced?

K.M.: I'm a secularist, so I refuse any political manipulation of religion. Islam has always been used in Algeria to justify one measure or another, by the government as well as by a part of the opposition. Boumediene did this to legitimize the agrarian revolution and the socialist management of enterprises, among other things. I think I've said enough about Chadli. For a long period during the 1970s and 1980s, the Communist Party militated in favor of the "Islam of the poor," a "progressive Islam." As for the F.I.S. ... It is not secularism that endangers Islam and its believers, but all the games that are played with Islam to legitimize the actions of a government. It is not up to politicians to explain and judge those actions, because they would invest the process with partisan stakes. Rather, it is up to civil society to pass judgment. Professor Stambouli, a prestigious Algerian scholar of Islam, published some remarkable work on that subject. That's undoubtedly why the fundamentalists assassinated him in August 1994.

E.S.: Is Algeria ready to listen to a discourse on secularism?

K.M.: Secularism is the result of a slow historical process that went hand in hand with the emergence of the individual and the citizen. This didn't happen without some crises and violence. The [Catholic] Church in France defended itself fiercely. It did not concede to secularism: the Church was fought by men and women who were initially in the minority before they convinced anyone.

Why should it be different for Algeria? Why should anyone claim that secularism is impossible in my country, under the pretext that you can't just wave a magic wand and make it appear? I am convinced that, although it may be difficult to say that Algeria is a society of citizens, it is, on the other hand, impossible to claim that it is a community of believers. The debate is not over the incompatibilities between Islam and secularism, because secularization in no way implies the destruction of religion. Rather, it is a question of determining what sort of state we want to construct: a state based on divine law or a state based on rights. I believe the current conditions favor the emergence of the individual and the citizen, more than has ever been true in the past. We're experiencing the painful genesis of those concepts, at this very moment. For there is another possible interpretation of what is happening today in Algeria, and I am surprised that almost no one has proposed it, with the notable exception of an Algerian jurist, Nouredine Saadi.

E.S.: What is that interpretation?

K.M.: In the face of fundamentalism, we Algerians are led to ask ourselves these essential questions: Is Islam the source of all our troubles—in other words, is Islamism integral to Islam? And how can we get out of that impasse? As soon as a society starts to reflect on questions like that, and to resist extremism passively or actively, the ultimate response can only be secularism, at least for a part of that society. For this debate is grounded in what is unique about Algeria: our country was structured on French republicanism for a century, and our society was indelibly marked by that experience.

E.S.: In the meantime, Algeria has chosen a form of resistance ...

K.M.: Yes, as you can see every day in Algeria, resistance is a popular reality that is directed as much against fundamentalism as it is against the regime. Villages are organizing their own defense, and networks of solidarity have been created ... The members of the resistance are the millions of citizens who brave death threats from the armed groups of the F.I.S., who confront corrupt officials and force them to resign, and who continue to go to work. They are also, of course, the female nurses, teachers, and students who simply go where they have to go without putting on a veil. Shouldn't we use the term heroism to speak about journalists and other women and men who work to ensure that some form of public speech continues to exist? It is thanks to all these figures of freedom, whether they be anonymous or in the spotlight, that Algeria has not collapsed.

E.S.: There are resistant villages all over Kabylia*. That's no coincidence. Isn't there a danger that the Kabyles may secede?

K.M.: Even if the resistance did, indeed, begin in the villages of Kabylia, and vigilance committees appeared there in October 1993, the phenomenon reached several other regions, like those of Jijel, Medea, and El-Asnam. It has since spread throughout the entire country. Wherever it is, resistance has the same objective: to prevent pillaging, the kidnapping or raping of women, and assassinations, using weapons if necessary. In Kabylia, this isn't a question of a tribal or regional conflict. But every time Kabylia undertakes an action, even if it is repeated elsewhere, somebody brings up the specter of secession. It's exasperating. This region paid dearly for the liberation of all of Algeria during the war of independence, and I challenge anyone to produce a single declaration claiming Kabyle autonomy or secession. On March 8 of last year, I traveled to Igoujdal, the first village to have mounted an armed resistance to the terrorist assaults that took place in July 1994, in order to celebrate International Women's Day. I met many women and men from the resistance, and listened to them closely: they never talked about a "Kabyle solution," they only spoke about the fate of Algeria ... History teaches us that when an ideology calls for some form of purifying segregation—as is true of the F.I.S.—only resistance and an insistence on democratic, republican values can counter it. I know that it is not easy to refuse fundamentalism while also opposing the government, but I prefer that particular difficulty to the chaos that would ensue from an alliance between the army and the F.I.S.

E.S.: In your opinion, is there a civil war going on in Algeria today?

K.M.: Certainly not. The violence runs through all of society and touches every family, but it does not divide two regions, or two ethnic groups, or two different religions. Nor is it a question of a simple conflict between the army and the F.I.S. The people who are shot down are not just the police and the military on one side, and the fundamentalist militants on the other, but also tens of thousands of unarmed civilians who are not involved in any camp. As

André Glucksmann put it, "This is not a civil war, but a war against civilians."

E.S.: Do you still believe that the government wants to have a dialogue with the F.I.S.? After the army tried to negotiate with Madani and Benhadj*, it apparently broke off relations with them. Benhadj was even sent to the South recently ...

K.M.: From the moment that Zeroual, a retired general, was called upon to serve as Minister of Defense, and then designated president in January 1994, he has tried to negotiate with the F.I.S. To that end, he liberated some of its leaders so that they could contact the armed groups. He lightened the conditions of detention for Madani and Benhadj, who were placed in a state-run residence where they had a fax machine and telephone at their disposal, as well as the possibility of receiving visitors. Zeroual was on his way to sharing power with these leaders, when a second clan in the army intervened to stop him. In my opinion, the F.I.S. didn't give certain generals sufficient guarantees for their own survival. That's why I fear that negotiations will resume, as soon as this handful of officials has received assurances on their own fate. The only objective of the Rome accords was to allow the F.I.S. and the army to find some grounds for agreement. More than a "peace" plan, it's the continuation of war in a different form.

E.S.: How would you define the Algerian impasse?

K.M.: I'd sum it up in a single sentence: no citizen in Algeria today trusts his leaders. And this regime wants to force us to accept the logic of "it's me or chaos." The fundamentalist camp, for its part, is guilty of the same sort of blackmail in that it presents itself as the only alternative to the crisis, using the same slogan: "It's me or chaos." What underlies the current impasse is precisely that Algerians, caught in a stranglehold, stuck between these two ultimatums, absolutely refuse to choose. People observing Algeria from outside the country don't understand this attitude well. It represents neither silence nor paralysis. Rather, it testifies to the Algerians' extreme lucidness and great wisdom, which, up to now, have allowed us to keep our tragic situation from become organic or inborn, as has happened in Lebanon or Yugoslavia. Although a good number of the ingredients for an explosion of that sort are present, it has not occurred, because the Algerian people don't want it to.

E.S.: So, if I understand you correctly, you're saying that the Algerian people are resolute? Does that mean, in your view, that there's no risk that they'll be brought to their knees?

K.M.: It is, indeed, the people, and not the F.I.S., who are resolute. Unfortunately, that doesn't mean that no one will try to subjugate the Algerian people. In the climate of terror that has been imposed by the armed groups of the F.I.S., the population must face a very difficult economic reality, which is aggravated by the draconian programs of the International Monetary Fund. A carton of milk today costs about $1.65, when the minimum wage is only about seventy dollars a month. The severe devaluation of the dinar caused a collapse in buying power, and the privatization plans that have been announced have triggered the risk of layoffs. A social explosion is latent, and the government is well aware of it. But because it is not any more able today than in the past to respond to this crisis with intelligent management, it will resort to repression. Now, the government is also aware that the F.I.S. will not hesitate to exploit popular discontent to swell its ranks. The possibility that an alliance will form between one military clan and the supporters of *Dawla islamia* [an Islamic state] therefore strikes me as very probable—all the more so, given that there would be something in it for many people: the regime, which would stay in office by sharing power; the F.I.S., which would finally gain access to state affairs; and the rest of the august members of the Rome assembly, who would certainly get a few scraps out of it. What a dream situation for the I.M.F., which would see its programs applied as soon as any popular protest was snuffed out!

E.S.: To get out of the impasse, the Algerian government has proposed presidential elections for next July [1996].[1] Are you ready to participate in them, and under what conditions?

K.M.: I will participate, if they are really free this time, and if they lead up to a democratic process that has never taken place. This supposes that any woman or man can go vote without pressure or threats of any sort. The armed groups must, therefore, necessarily be disbanded. The candidates must be assured full access to the media. All the parties must commit themselves to re-

---

1. See "Recent Elections in Algeria" in the Glossary.

specting the rotation of office, pluralism, and democratic values. The religious parties will have to renounce their practice of presenting their candidates as the spokesmen of God on earth. The electoral rolls will have to be reviewed. The rolls that we now have available date from the time when the F.I.S. held municipal authority. Moreover, more than seven hundred town halls or county offices were, along with their archives, destroyed by the terrorists, and a new census will have to be done on the people who fled the terror. The Algerians are traumatized by the 1991 elections and will have to be reassured. But how can one inspire confidence in women who are still living under the reign of the Family Code?

E.S.: Do you think you'll be able to resume a normal life soon, Khalida?

K.M.: Unfortunately, I'm afraid not. All you have to do is consider how many women were shot down during the cursed month of March 1995. The victims included schoolgirls, high school students, and young women who were nine months pregnant. They were killed just because they were women and were there, outside, at a bus stop, a market, or schoolroom. Aren't we still in the crazy logic of "You die for what you are"?

E.S.: Isn't it enough to make you despair?

K.M.: My cry is desperate, surely. How could it be otherwise, in the face of so much horror and injustice, in the face of this coalition of evil and terror? Elisabeth, I'm dealing—we're dealing—with an Islamist International. What inequality, what disequilibrium! Is my battle lost? Certainly not. Every day, it is a bit more comforted and sustained by a formidable support network that is finding its way and trying to get organized. The letter "To Algerian Women" which Jean Daniel published in *Le Nouvel Observateur* on the occasion of International Women's Day, March 8, 1995, is in my view revealing—or, better, groundbreaking. It is the necessary trigger for the formation and emergence of a "democratic International" for which I have been calling with all my might since 1993, from Vienna, where the Tribunal on Violence Toward Women was held. At the time, I had the impression that I was preaching in the desert. Today, the quality of the signatories to that letter, and the power, justness, and sincerity of its contents—a magnificent expression of the resistance of my people—strengthen me, uplift me, and keep me from sinking into despair.

Thank you to all those men and women. Thank you from the Algeria of Katia, who was shot down at the age of seventeen for having said "no" to the veil, and from the Algeria of Kheïra, who, despite having been gang-raped, still found the courage to testify.

E.S.: So you won't give in?

K.M.: Never.

Epilogue: Algeria Today

Almost three years have passed since these interviews were conducted. During that time Algeria has lived through a situation that is, in a sense, schizophrenic.

On the one hand, the massacres perpetrated by the armed Islamic groups against the civilian population have intensified to an unbearable degree: thousands of women, children, and babies have had their throats slit in Algeria's villages and even in the suburbs of Algiers. The government's efforts to suppress the fundamentalist terrorists have failed to put an end to the terror, for two reasons. First, those efforts have, at times, been made without regard to the fact that these religious fanatics are surrounded by an entire entourage; that approach has only reinforced the solidarity that exists among the fundamentalists. Second, the government has quite often ordered the police and military forces not to intervene during the massacres; it has done that purely for strategic reasons, to further the objective of turning Algerians away from Islamism once and for all.

On the other hand, while the horror was mounting, the elections that had been planned took place as scheduled: presidential elections were held in November 1995, followed by elections on the constitution in October 1996, legislative elections in June 1997, and municipal elections in October of the same year. The goal of these elections was to establish an institutional apparatus that was supposedly democratic—a façade designed, in fact, to reinforce the military government and to satisfy the hypocritical demands for formal liberty that had been made by the great international monetary institutions, the World Bank and the International Monetary Fund. In reality, the results of each of these

elections were rigged, right under the noses of the foreign observers mandated by the United Nations or the Organization of
Arab Unity, without prompting any outcry from those organizations, nor from the various Western governments involved. President Liamine Zeroual* emerged each time as the uncontestable
victor, but only because his entire tactic consisted in manipulating
the ballots in order to control the Algerian political landscape as
he pleased. He thus deliberately diminished the electoral score
and the audience of the R.C.D.*, amplified those of the F.F.S.*—a
party in the process of collapsing, and the R.C.D.'s enemy
brother—and propelled Hamas*, the so-called "moderate" Islamist party of Cheik Nahnah, which openly advocates establishing
an Islamic state through elections.

In this extremely difficult context, Khalida Messaoudi has stuck
to the policy that she defined throughout these interviews. She
played a considerable role in ensuring that the R.C.D. was on the
ballot for the presidential elections of 1995, just as she had emphasized in our interviews. Moreover, she agreed to be the
spokesperson for Saïd Sadi*, head of the R.C.D., during those
elections. "My positions on women and the Family Code* were
well known. Finally, for the first time in the history of a Muslim
country, a political leader chose to have at his side a woman who
had followed a feminist path, knowing full well what that represented. Having been told that my primary identity would be respected and my political position assured, and that I would be able
to continue the good fight for secularism and equal rights in all
areas, I wasn't about to refuse what the R.C.D. had proposed!"

Of course, accepting this position might have meant breaking
the principle Khalida herself had defined: a feminist should be independent in relation to any and all parties. That is why she immediately offered to resign from her post as president of her
association (the A.I.T.D.F.*). Her resignation was accepted but
temporarily postponed, through a unanimous vote, because there
was no one available who had the stature necessary to take her
place. In spite of that, the results of the presidential elections were
immensely disappointing for the camp of radical democrats, for
they had believed Zeroual's claim that he wanted to reform the
system, when all he really wanted was to persuade them to support
the ballot.

Being played for fools in this way prompted them to boycott the vote on the new constitution that later took place, in 1996. Islam, it is true, was recognized in this constitution as the state religion, and Berber culture—including the Berber language—was carefully suppressed. Moreover, a two-house system was going to be set up in which the second legislative branch, composed exclusively of members who had been coopted by the government, would necessarily be all-powerful.

Sadi's party, however, decided to resume its place on the political chessboard during the legislative elections of 1997. Khalida Messaoudi explains: "From the moment that many Algerians are forced into exile, it becomes incumbent on those who remain to stay alive—both in the literal sense of the term and in the political sense. Staying on the sidelines of the new Assembly and the forum it offered us, despite everything, would have been tantamount to shutting ourselves down and leaving the path open for a very long time to both the corrupted military government and fundamentalists of all sorts. The democratic pole could not disintegrate." That is how Khalida, second on the R.C.D.'s list, became a representative for Algiers. What an extraordinary adventure for this secular, democratic feminist, who won in a district that the F.I.S.* had carried hands down in 1990 and 1991!

In this Assembly, the new deputy is relentless, particularly concerning the situation of women. "I am ready," she asserts, "to form an alliance with anyone who will defend the repeal of the twenty-two unacceptable articles of the Family Code. And I will do so regardless of the R.C.D.'s opinion; and, in any case, the members of the R.C.D. know full well that I am the one who sets the policy on this subject."

The fact remains that Algeria is at an impasse. It is an impasse of violence, and it is difficult, for the time being, to see how the violence could be stopped other than by giving in completely to the Islamists. The Algerian government has already given them the mosques, schools, courts, and women. It has even, within the government, placed privatization and industry in their hands. Because the government truly wishes to promote Islamism, but an Islamism free of terrorism, the very real repression it exerts in the area of arms has no hope of succeeding. It is not enough to fight a totalitarian system physically; one must also attack its ideology, and do so in the halls of power and proselytism, rather than abandoning them to it. The paradox of the Algerian situation—a paradox that still misleads observers, commentators, and great powers to the same degree—thus remains just as acute as ever: namely, there is only a tactical difference between the government and the fundamentalists, and supporting one or the other camp amounts to nothing more than favoring form over substance. In that sense, it remains true that the interruption of the electoral process of 1991 was necessary—it was the assassination of Boudiaf that brought an end to the evolution toward democracy that had been underway—whereas increased repression has no justification. It is thus probable that Algeria has bloody days ahead, for it is now in a kind of status quo. Only the Algerians will bear the brunt of this status quo, and only they will be able to extricate themselves from it.

Elisabeth Schemla

Glossary

Acronyms

A.I.T.D.F. (*Association Indépendante pour le Triomphe des Droits des Femmes*): Independent Association for the Triumph of Women's Rights, founded and led by Khalida Messaoudi.

A.L.N. (*Armée de Libération Nationale*): National Liberation Army. Led Algeria's war of independence against France (1954–62).

A.P.C. (*Assemblées Populaires Communales*): Popular Communal Assemblies.

C.C.N. (*Conseil Consultatif National*): National Advisory Council.

F.A.F. (*Fraternité des Algériens en France*): Brotherhood of Algerians in France, an organization closely tied to the F.I.S.

F.F.S. (*Front des Forces Socialistes*): Front of Socialist Forces, an opposition party created by Aït Ahmed in 1963.

F.I.S. (*Front Islamique du Salut*): Islamic Salvation Front. The F.I.S. is an umbrella organization for a number of fundamentalist subgroups that, although not necessarily united, all seek to create a single Islamic state in which Islamic law is strictly applied. Since the F.I.S. was banned in 1992, the fundamentalist movement has fractured. See also Benhadj; Madani.

F.L.N. (*Front de Libération Nationale*): National Liberation Front. The F.L.N., which grew out of the national movement that led to Algeria's independence in 1962, had sole control of the Algerian government from 1962 until 1991, when it was humiliated in legislative elections and fell from power. The recently created R.N.D. party is considered by many to be a "neo"-F.L.N. See also Ben Bella; Boumediene; Chadli; P.P.A.-M.T.L.D.

G.I.A. (*Groupe Islamique Armê*): Armed Islamic Group.

H.C.E. (*Haut Comité d'Etat*): High State Committee.

M.D.A. (*Mouvement pour la Démocratie*): Movement for Democracy in Algeria, headed by Ahmed Ben Bella.

M.E.I. (*Mouvement pour l'Etat Islamique*): Movement for the Islamic State, led by Saïd Makhloufi. The M.E.I., a branch of the F.I.S., issued the death decree against Khalida Messaoudi in 1993.

M.I.A. (*Mouvement Islamique Algérien*): Algerian Islamic Movement, created by Mustafa Bouyali.

M.J.A. (*Mouvement des Journalistes Algériens*): Algerian Journalists' Movement.

M.N.A. (*Mouvement National Algérien*): National Algerian Movement, created by Messali Hadj.

M.P.R. (*Mouvement pour la République*): Movement for the Republic. A secular organization whose current vice-president is Khalida Messaoudi.

P.P.A.-M.T.L.D. (*Parti du Peuple Algérien—Mouvement pour le Triomphe des Libertés Démocratiques*): Party of the Algerian People—Movement for the Triumph of Political Liberties. Founded in 1937 and led by Messali Hadj, the P.P.A. was the first nationalist party to call for Algerian independence from France. It was outlawed in 1939. After emerging from several years of house arrest, Messali Hadj joined with other P.P.A. militants to create the M.T.L.D. The M.T.L.D. produced the original founders of the F.L.N. and helped to trigger the Algerian war of independence in 1954.

P.T.T. (*Postes et Télécommunications*): Postal and Telecommunication Services.

R.C.D. (*Rassemblement pour la Culture et la Démocratie*): Rally for Culture and Democracy, an opposition party led by Saïd Sadi that promotes secular, republican values. Khalida Messaoudi is presently an R.C.D. deputy in the National Assembly.

R.N.D. (*Rassemblement National Démocratique*): National Democratic Union. Considered to be the party of President Zeroual, the R.N.D. was created at the beginning of 1997 and won the legislative elections held in June of the same year. It has pan-Arabic, Islamo-baasist* tendencies similar to those of the old F.L.N. The acronym R.N.D. may have been deliberately chosen to create confusion with the opposition party known as the R.C.D.

Sonacom (*Société Nationale de Construction Mécanique*): National Society for Mechanical Construction.

U.N.F.A. (*Union Nationale des Femmes Algériennes*): National Union of Algerian Women, an F.L.N. organization.

Algerian and French Terms

Aïd: a holiday that commemorates Abraham's sacrifice.

Assemblée-croupion ("Rump Assembly"): adaptation of the term "rump parliament," which is a legislature having only a remnant of its former members, as, e.g., because of expulsions, and hence regarded as unrepresentative and without authority. Messaoudi uses it to refer to a parliament in which all representatives were F.L.N. members.

baraka: luck, grace, supernatural blessing.

burnous (from the Kabyle word *varnous*): a full-length cloak with a hood, woven out of very fine white or brown wool, worn by Berber men in Kabylia and in the Rif region of Morocco.

chaabi: very popular brand of traditional Algerian folk music, characteristic of the region of Algiers.

charia: canon law of Islam; refers to the entire body of texts formed by the Koran, the *hadiths*, and the exegeses of various religious authorities and imams. The term is also used to describe the application of Islamic law, as in Saudi Arabia or Iran.

chorba: a lamb, tomato, and coriander soup.

Code communal: Code imposed by the French in the 1930s to control the Algerian population. It also included provisions for compulsory education of girls and boys.

daâwa: proselytism.

Family Code: law primarily concerned with the rights of women, which it severely restricts. Also known as the "Code sur le statut personnel" ("Code on Personal Status"). The Family Code, first proposed in 1981, met with vigorous protest from women's groups like the A.I.T.D.F. but was nonetheless passed into law by the F.L.N. in 1984.

fatwa: formal legal opinion given by a canon lawyer (*mufti*); often entails a legal justification of a practice like the condemnation of a person or practice.

fota: a piece of cloth, usually in red, yellow, and black, worn on the hips by Kabyle women. It is also what women wear in a public bath.

hadiths: the words of the Prophet.

hammam: Turkish bath; a type of sauna.

hidjab: literally, "curtain." *Hidjab* is a word with many meanings, now often used as a synonym for modest Islamic dress for women. An article of clothing imported from the Arab East, in Algeria it means a headscarf often worn with a loose gown. According to the fundamentalists, it should allow nothing but a woman's hands and face to be seen.

hisba: a system in which one must account for every private or public act.

Islamo-baasist: in favor of Arabization (rather than French-language education) and of Islamist religio-political beliefs. "Baasist" refers to the Baath Party, a leftist, nationalist, chauvinistic party.

Kaâba: the black stone of Mecca, one of the holiest places in Islam, known for being a place of reconciliation and sanctuary.

khol'â: a practice that allows a woman to divorce on the condition that she give up any claim to alimony.

"Ma neshakouch felfel ekhel neshakou Raïs Fhel" ("We don't need black pepper, we need a decent leader"): The term *raïs* is Arabic for "president." This slogan is a pun in Algerian Arabic with several meanings. First, black pepper is gray and white, and may refer here to President Chadli's hair. Second, black pepper is an imported foodstuff, a luxury item that requires foreign currency. Chadli's economic strategy was to privatize and import everything. "Raïs Fhel" means not merely a "decent president" but, through the addition of *fhel*, a "real man" or "macho leader." One might, therefore, paraphrase the slogan as follows: we're prepared to live less well (with shortages of imported items) but with a real president who prepares for our future.

marabout: Whereas the word can mean "preacher," "Muslim clerk," or "charlatan" in West Africa, in Kabylia it refers to someone who belongs to the noble caste, a descendant of the *Al mooravids*, the Moorish dynasty that once ruled Spain. Messaoudi uses it in the latter sense.

moudjahidin (masculine singular: *moudjahid*): fighters in a liberation army. In its religious sense, this term refers to fighters for the faith against nonbelievers. During the Algerian war of independence the name was given to those who fought the French.

moudjahidat (feminine singular: *moudjahida*): women resistance fighters.

ouléma: plural of *alim*, which means "scholar." In Algeria the term *ouléma* generally refers to religious scholars. The "Association of Ouléma" founded in 1936 was a jointly religious and political movement whose members supported French colonialism and sought assimilation for "evolved" Muslims like themselves. See also Ben Badis.

oumma: the community.

pasdahan (or *pasdaharan*): morals militia in Iran, famous for harassing women who show too much ankle or wisps of hair.

raï: Oran-based, world-beat music that combines traditional musical genres (Algerian, Andalusian, and rural) with technological innovations such as synthesizers and electronic magnification. It appeared in the 1970s and reached Europe and the United States in the 1980s.

Sunna: the Tradition of the Prophet.

sura: a chapter in the Koran.

zakat: legal alms-giving that is incumbent on every Muslim.

zaouadj el moutaâ, or "marriage of joy": a practice that consists in forcing women to marry temporarily.

zaouïa: an institution, run by a prominent marabout, that is devoted particularly to teaching reading, writing, religion, science, and geography. This institution, typical of the Maghreb (Morocco, Algeria, Tunisia) is very decentralized and local. It is opposed, in both its mode of functioning and its social role, to the centralized, hegemonic structures typical of the Middle East or Iran. The zaouïa were generally created between the tenth and twelfth centuries by marabout families and are still run by the descendants of those families.

Sociohistorical References (Names, Places, and Events)

Aït Ahmed: a Kabyle who led the F.F.S. and strove to establish democracy in Algeria. Ahmed was arrested after creating the F.F.S. in 1963; he was condemned to death by the F.L.N. government and then exiled. He returned to Algeria in 1989.

Algerian Hamas: the second Islamic party in Algeria, after the F.I.S. Considered "moderate." Also known as the M.S.P. (*Mouvement pour la Société et pour la Paix*, or Movement for Society and Peace), it is presently led by Mahfoud Nahnah.

Aurès: mountainous region east of Algiers and south of Constantine.

Abdelhamid Ben Badis: president of the "Association of Ouléma," which he founded in 1936. Although he and the other religious leaders involved in this association argued in favor of cultural and religious autonomy during the colonial era, they opposed Algerian independence and favored assimilation with the French. Ben Badis advocated a fundamentalist brand of Islam and disapproved of local Muslim practices.

Ahmed Ben Bella: first Prime Minister of independent Algeria, who served from 1963 until he was overthrown by his minister of Defense, Houari Boumediene, in 1965. He was the leader of those who favored an Arab Algeria, and thus opposed movements like the F.F.S. It was under Ben Bella's reign that the F.L.N.'s one-party regime was imposed.

Ali Benhadj: second in command in the F.I.S., notable for his misogyny. Responsible for a huge Islamist demonstration held in Bab el-Oued in October, 1988, which was bloodily suppressed by the Chadli government.

Bigeard and Massu: two French generals famous for "restoring order" through the use of terrorism and torture during the Battle of Algiers in 1956–57.

Mohamed Boudiaf: member of the group of twenty-two militants who started the Algerian revolution (1954–62). President of Algeria from January 1992 until June of the same year, when he was slain while making a televised speech in which he condemned official government corruption and stressed the need to compile legal dossiers against the nation's former rulers (the F.L.N. and its accomplice, the F.I.S.).

Djamila Bouhired: legendary Algerian moudjahida. During the 1960s, Simone de Beauvoir wrote a book entitled *Pour Djamila Bouhired* in her defense.

Houari Boumediene: president of Algeria from 1965, when he led a coup d'état against Ben Bella, until his death in 1978.

Chadli Ben Djedid: president of Algeria from 1978 to 1991, when he and the F.L.N. fell from power.

Chaouia: Berbers of the Aurès region. Algeria's major Berber groups are the Kabyles of the Kabylie Mountains, and the Chaouia of the Aurès mountains.

En-Nahda (or Ennahda): literally, "renewal" or "renaissance." An Islamist political party led by Djaballah, one of the signatories of the Rome, 1995 accords.

Jules Ferry: French lawyer, politician, and writer (1832–93). In his various capacities he introduced major reforms in France's public school system: secularism, free education, mandatory attendance in primary school, and the extension of secondary education to girls. Ferry also helped to establish freedom of assembly, of the press, and of unions in France, and to reorganize local government. Lastly, he greatly expanded France's colonial policy: he oversaw the transformation of Tunisia into a French protectorate, the colonization of Madagascar, the conquest of the lower Congo, and the conquest of Tonkin.

Messali Hadj: labor union activist who led the M.N.A., the P.P.A., and then the M.T.L.D.

Louisa Hannoun: Trotskyist leader, president of the *Parti des Travailleurs* (Workers Party).

Islam in Algeria: the primary form of Islam practiced in North Africa is Malekism, one of the five branches of Sunnism. Sunnites, who make up one of the two great sects of Muslims (the other sect being that of the Shiites), accept the Sunna as an authoritative supplement to the Koran. In many Berber areas, such as Kabylia, a mixture of Judeo-pagano-Malekism is still practiced, and regional traditions and the word of local sages take precedence over religious doctrine.

Kabyle, Kabylia: a region distinguished from the rest of the Mahgreb by its language (Kabyle), culture, and political orientation. Despite all the repression it has endured since Algeria became independent, Kabylia has adamantly refused to be Arabized. It has democratic institutions that have been in place for centuries, as well as a long tradition of opposing centralized power and resisting colonialism. Kabylia is also Algeria's primary Francophone region (comparable to Québec in Canada).

Ouacini Laaredj (or Waciny Larej): anti-establishment Arabic-language author, despised by the fundamentalists for his secular, democratic beliefs. Laaredj's novel *La Gardienne des ombres* has been translated from the Arabic in *Algérie: Littérature/Action* 3–4 (1996).

Language in Algeria: the four primary languages spoken in Algeria are classical Arabic, French, Algerian Arabic (a mixture of French, Arabic, and Berber, also called "Algerian" or *faraber*), and Berber. Kabyle is one of the main spoken forms of Berber. The written culture of Algeria has always been in the language of the colonizer: Saint Augustine, whose native tongue was Berber, wrote in Latin, the language of the region's Roman colonizers; Ibn Khaldoun—Averroës, the twelfth-century philosopher—wrote in the language of the Arab colonizers; and contemporary authors like Kateb Yacine write in French, the language inherited from Algeria's last colonial era.

Abassi Madani: F.I.S. president and former member of the F.L.N. Among the most reactionary of Islamist leaders.

Recent elections in Algeria: The presidential elections of July 1996 were won by General Zeroual, the Army candidate. These elections were followed by legislative elections in June, 1997. Despite the election fraud that gave most of the legislative seats to the F.L.N.-R.N.D., Khalida Messaoudi was elected representative in a district of Algiers. She is, however, still condemned to death.

Rome meeting of January 1995: a meeting held in Rome under the auspices of the Catholic association San Egidio, which sought to bring together all Algeria's opposing political parties in order to stop the high death toll, estimated in 1995 at 30,000 dead. General Zeroual, then head of the H.C.E. (and not yet elected President) condemned the meeting, thereby dooming it to failure.

Saïd Sadi: militant who organized the Berber uprising of 1980, helped create the original Algerian League for Human Rights in 1985, and founded the R.C.D. in 1989.

Jacques Vergès: prominent French lawyer who specializes in political trials. Husband of Djamila Bouhired.

Kateb Yacine: French-language playwright, banned by the F.L.N. and the Islamists, whose writings include *L'Homme aux sandales de caoutchouc* and *Nedjma.*

Ali Yahya: lawyer and one-time minister in the Boumediene government. He participated in the creation of the Algerian League for Human Rights but later became an ally of the fundamentalists.

General Liamine Zeroual: retired Army general; president of Algeria since 1994.

Biographical Profile

Khalida Messaoudi

President of the A.I.T.D.F.* (Independent Association for the
Triumph of Women's Rights)
Vice President of the M.P.R.* (Movement for the Republic)
Elected deputy to the Algerian National Assembly
Sentenced to death by Islamic fundamentalists

Education

She studied political economy at the Institut des Travaux et de la
Planification (1977–79) and mathematics at the Ecole Normale
Supérieure in Algiers (1978–83), where she received a bachelor's
degree and a master's degree in mathematics.

Awards

She has received several awards from international women's rights
groups and human rights organizations in Europe and various
third-world countries. Most recently (October 1997), she was
awarded the first Prix International "Alexander Langer" from the
Association Pro Europa, a human rights foundation in Italy, as a
tribute to her struggle for human rights in Algeria.

Political Activities

1980–81: One of the original founders of "Collectif Femmes," an
independent women's rights organization. She organized and led
demonstrations against the F.L.N.*-controlled government and
the fundamentalists to protest the "Family Code*." She was one of
two women arrested for demonstrating in 1981 (cf. "Les Algériennes et la lutte," *Les Temps Modernes* [July–August 1982]).

1985: Founder and president of the "Association pour l'Egalité
des Droits entre les Femmes et les Hommes" (Association for
Equal Rights Between Women and Men).

1989: Founder and president of the A.I.T.D.F.* (Independent Association for the Triumph of Women's Rights), an organization recognized by the F.L.N. in March, 1989. Two weeks later, the fundamentalist party F.I.S.* (Islamic Salvation Front) was also officially recognized.

1990: On March 8, she led the International Women's Day march in Algiers. On March 22, she debated Abassi Madani, leader of the fundamentalist F.I.S. party, on Algerian national television. In preparation for the debate, she defied five of the interdictions imposed on women by the Islamists: she went to the hairdresser, curled her red hair, applied lipstick and makeup, wore pants, and wore her hair on her shoulders rather than covering her head with a scarf. She defied two more interdictions during the debate: she looked directly at Madani rather than lowering her eyes, and she questioned him in French and *Algerian* Arabic. Madani refused to reply and said in classical Arabic that she did not represent Algerian women.

1992: She led a march against Islamic fundamentalists (cf. "Algiers Women Demonstrate Against the Fundamentalists," *New York Times,* January 10, 1992, p. A3). She was one of six women among the sixty people appointed to the C.C.N.* (National Advisory Council), an interim congress created by President Boudiaf, who would be assassinated six months later.

1993: Several members of the C.C.N. were assassinated. Messaoudi received numerous death threats before being officially condemned to death by Islamic fundamentalists through an irreversible *fatwa.** As a result, she quit her teaching job in the spring of 1993, went underground, and has been living in hiding ever since.

1993–95: While still in hiding, she was interviewed by Paul Morin of French Canadian CBC TV, twice by the French television station Antenne 2 (including an appearance on "L'Heure de vérité," a one-hour program similar to CBS's *Sixty Minutes*), by the *Toronto Star* ("Fugitive Caught in a Crossfire Between Military and Islamists," Dec. 15, 1994, p. A25), and by *Le Nouvel Observateur* ("Le voile, c'est notre étoile jaune," Sept. 22–26, 1994, pp. 11–12). She also published an article ("La Nouvelle Inquisition," *Les Temps*

Modernes [January 1995], pp. 213–20) and appeared on the cover of the French news magazine *Le Point*, which devoted an article to her ("Khalida Messaoudi, féministe algérienne," April 1, 1995, pp. 35–38).

1994: In April, *Etabsira*, the news bulletin published by the F.I.S. in London, announced a failed assassination attempt against her, commenting that "she won't have to wait for long." In June, during the March for Democracy organized by the M.P.R.*, she was once again the object of an assassination attempt in which two people were killed and seventy wounded, including Messaoudi (cf. "L'Horreur à Alger," *Paris Match*, July 14, 1994).

1995: Her autobiography *Une Algérienne debout* was published in April by Flammarion. It was reviewed by Elisabeth Badinter in *Le Nouvel Observateur* (April 27, 1995, p. 66); Badinter described Messaoudi and the other women of the Algerian resistance as potential recipients of the Nobel Peace Prize.

1996: *Une donna in piedi*, the Italian translation of *Une Algérienne debout*, came out. In March, Messaoudi traveled to Israel (she is the only political figure from Algeria to have visited Israel, because the Algerian government and the Islamists still do not recognize that country). In April, she published a tribute to Simone de Beauvoir ("Hommage au Castor," *Le Monde*, April 19, 1996, p. vii). Beauvoir's memoir *La Force de l'âge* [*The Prime of Life*] remains one of Messaoudi's favorite books, along with Jorge Semprun's *Literature or Life*, which she considers an "antidote against despair" (Semprun is a survivor of the Buchenwald concentration camp).

1997: In February, she escaped another attempt on her life, this time in Lille, France; the incident was reported on the Antenne 2 program "Les Réseaux islamistes en Europe." On April 23, she appeared on a special edition of Bernard Pivot's television program *Bouillon de culture* entitled "La Résistance algérienne." In June, she was elected to the Algerian National Assembly under the banner of the R.C.D.* (Rally for Culture and Democracy), a secular republican opposition party led by Dr. Saïd Sadi*.

Despite her election to the National Assembly, Messaoudi's death sentence remains in effect.

Death Sentence for Khalida Messaoudi Sent by the F.I.S. on June 12, 1993

In the Name of Mild and Merciful God
The Movement for the Islamic State [M.E.I.*]
On behalf of the soldiers of God, the allies and guardians of the Merciful One, to the collaborators of the Despot, the allies and guardians of Satan:
A Communiqué and Warning
First Name: Khalida
Last Name: Messaoudi

The men of the Djihad in Algeria have taken the path toward the construction of a state of Islam, a state where there is no other God than Allah and Mohammed is his prophet. They have declared war on the despots whose opposition to Islam and its people has been proven, and they only understand the language of arms.

On this basis, and to have a clear conscience before God and History, the men of the Islamic Djihad address a solemn warning to all those who think they can rise up against the soldiers of God and who were, in fact, raised in the arms of the Despot, offering him assistance—in whatever form and place it may be—against the movement of the Islamic Djihad.

The men of the Islamic Djihad therefore say to these unbelieving collaborators of the Despot, that the striking force and the length of the Islamic military arm is growing every day—with God's help—and that it is able, now more than ever, to pursue all of these traitors, renegades, and criminals, wherever they may be.

Nothing will stop the soldiers of God, who will pursue them and kill them, whether they are in their homes or in the street, whether they surround themselves with impregnable ramparts, or even if they cling to the curtains of the *Kaâba**. They [the collaborators] should, above all, not count on the protection of their Despot, for despots fall one after the other, from the smallest to the greatest. And they should know that their foreign supporters are not at all safe from the arm of the Islamic Djihad.

So, either you cease your opposition to the Islamic Djihad, or its violent tempest will carry you away.

This represents our first and last warning.

Know that he who warns is absolved and that you will have no further excuse after this communiqué.

[This is followed by the seal of the Movement for the Islamic State, led by Saïd Makhloufi.]